REFLECTIONS
Homes and History of Columbus, Mississippi

Text by Sylvia Higginbotham

Photography by Mark Coffey

Copyright 2001
Eugene B. Imes, Publisher
Columbus, Mississippi

Library of Congress
2001 130022

ISBN 0-9711554-0-2

Final Copy Editing - George Hazard,
Columbus, MS.

Book Design - Ariadne Alexoudis,
Lead Free Studio, Atlanta, GA.

Printed in China by Everbest Printing
Company through Four Colour Imports,
Louisville, KY.

Reflections

Homes and History of Columbus, Mississippi

Text By Sylvia Higginbotham

Photography By Mark Coffey

This book was made possible in part due to the cooperation and generosity of the people of Columbus, Mississippi, who own and care for the homes of history. The Columbus homes are not museums; they are residences which, through their existence, tell remarkable stories of the development of the American South.

Thanks to the work of the Columbus Historic Foundation and the dedicated historians who keep the organization active, outstanding antebellum mansions continue to welcome guests who appreciate their architectural heritage.

Thanks, too, to the Columbus Public Library, the Columbus-Lowndes Historical Society, the Preservation of Antiquities, and so many groups and individuals who share a commitment to preserving the region's rich heritage.

Featured Homes

Preface

$\infty\circ\infty$

Columbus, Mississippi, is a town where a feeling of permanence withstands the movement of time. Ask the locals to define that quality, and they'll say, "It's home. This is the way it's always been."

In this hectic world where changes occur faster than the speed of sound, it is indeed a pleasure to know that in some special places, things are still the way they've always been. Columbus is such a place, for traditions are honored here, and friendships are made to last a lifetime.

History is important here, and it, too, is sometimes revered. The history surrounding the origins of Memorial Day, which began in Columbus in 1866 as "Decoration Day," is a story we never get tired of telling. Decoration Day came about because of the generous nature of the women of Columbus, and the gracious deed that prompted the poignant poem, "The Blue and the Gray," set a standard for all who followed.

So often, history recounts hard facts. The events interspersed with wars and famine sometimes leave us with a sense of sadness. And even though history is very much a part of Columbus today —and the basis for the cherished traditions we hold so dear— this book will not dwell on the sadness of the past. Rather, it will feature the fanciful side of the way things were, from the ornate homes built by the early citizens, to the way they entertained with grand parties that lasted several days. After all, it took a while to get from place to place, and, once the guests arrived, they had to stay long enough to rest up for the return trip home.

The antebellum homes of Columbus serve as living history accounts of a different era, and they do so in full and vivid color. Purists appreciate the historic homes that have been painstakingly preserved —those which remain true to the integrity of the period and style in which the home was built, and there are many such structures here. Columbus is flush with fine examples of popular homes that still reflect the magnificent work of builders and craftsmen of the mid-1800s, among them Waverley, Riverview, White Arches, Rosedale, The Pratt Thomas Home, and so many more.

Throughout the South, we see homes that are grandiloquent in their cosmetic work and alterations, though what's left of the original structure may call upon the imagination. You won't see too much of that in Columbus, for maintaining architectural integrity is another cherished tradition. The general consensus appears to be that whatever alterations were and are made are commendable when one considers the alternatives: demolition.

True lovers of historic architecture must cringe when they travel through towns once rich in grand old homes and see instead a nightmare of drive-through food sellers and parking lots. Many of our Southern architectural treasures no longer exist, because someone mistook destruction for progress.

Interest in architectural preservation began in the 1970s, after the 1950s and 1960s had seen the demolition of many of the town's treasures, despite that tradition of reverence for the great works of the past. Thanks to the work and efforts of such dedicated preservationists as Ken P'Pool of the Mississippi Department of Archives and History, local architect Sam Kaye, AIA, local historian Carl Butler, and other members of the community who live in the heritage homes, much fact has been separated from fiction. Unfortunately, since few actual records were kept in the early days, years of handing stories down may have contributed to a bit of fanciful misinformation surrounding some of the homes.

The South and its architecture, so very well represented in Columbus, is so much more than the time-worn cliches of moonlight and magnolias, and mint juleps on the veranda, as suggested by films and novels. When historical records are not available to describe the lifestyle of the day, look to the houses. They document the social history of the time.

We think our book, "Reflections," is timely and necessary, and we hope it will encourage someone to look in amazement at the houses that serve as grand examples of pride in workmanship. Much of the fine work represents the skills of craftsmen who apprenticed for years before they began their life's work. We want to reaffirm that indeed, architecture is art, and we want to show that Columbus, Mississippi, has retained a remarkable collection of architectural art.

This book is not all-inclusive, for our town is rich in historic homes. The richness is seen not only in the antebellum mansions, but in vintage cottages, too. We've included a few of the most visible historic houses often referred to as cottages, for they, too, have important stories to tell. There are many outstanding structures not included here, though we hope to see them featured in other books or perhaps an update of this one. In researching the book, we found many discrepancies in available material concerning date of construction, builder, first owner, and more. Please know that we have made every effort to be accurate, though inaccuracies may inadvertently occur.

The homes on the following pages represent the styles and incorporate the significant history of the region, but if you really want to experience timeless treasures, drive through the old streets of historic Columbus, and see many grand mansions still standing tall and proud, the way they always have.

Gene Imes, Publisher
Sylvia Higginbotham, Author
Columbus, Mississippi. November, 2001

Reflections

Back in the early 1800s, settlers from the East Coast came westward in search of rich land and a better life. They found that the promised land was indeed available in the lush country along the Tombigbee River, but the land was already inhabited by Native Americans.

Hernando de Soto, that vagabond European explorer who reputedly traipsed through most every patch of land from Florida to the Mississippi River, was the first light-skinned person to appear in these parts. He made his trek through the region in 1540, with his entourage in tow. What a sight the travelers must have been for the Indians who had limited knowledge of other people. Several hundred years after the European adventurers departed, the American Indians followed suit, though their departure was not a festive occasion. Even though the chieftains sanctioned the move, it was a forced departure for the majority of the Indians who had harvested and hunted the fruits of the land.

The Chickasaw Indians inhabited the land east of the Tombigbee, while the Choctaws claimed the land to the west. Their largesse was not to last, for the East Coast people of the bold and aggressive new United States began the search for more and better land, and the new government helped them by slowly removing the Indian threat to advancement.

The first actual settlement in this region was established by the Spaniards in 1790 at Old Plymouth, also known as Old Choctaw or Cedar Log Fort. The government touted westward expansion, and after the War of 1812, there was a definite need for a military road to connect New Orleans and Nashville. The probable site was an existing Indian trail that ran through this area.

In 1816, the Chickasaw Treaty gave land on which Columbus now lies to the U.S. government, and a survey was soon under way to forge a great new road through the Indian land and wilderness. A military unit prepared the survey and reported their findings to then Major General Andrew Jackson, for whom the new Military Road was later named.

The Mayhew Mission to the Choctaw Indians came into being in 1817, when the Indians requested the presence of teachers and religious instructors who could help them learn the white man's ways. The American Board of Missions sent missionaries, who opened the Mayhew Mission School in 1820, with twelve students and $6,000 in annuities from the wealthy Choctaws. The basic curriculum was Bible, reading, writing, and arithmetic. Boys learned blacksmithing, carpentry, furniture making, bridge making, and farm work, while the girls learned housekeeping, sewing, knitting, weaving, and butter and cheese making. The mission had a Church of Christ on the premises by 1821; it was later received into the Presbyterian church. Today, all that's left of the Mayhew Mission is a cemetery.

The oldest documented section of Columbus, settled in 1817, is the downtown area. The central trade area was along Main Street, from the river hill to Fifth (Market) Street. Originally, frame buildings and small frame houses sprang up along the trade area. Once Columbus was chartered, frame structures began to be replaced by brick buildings, which were preferred for stability and as fire deterrents.

In the spring of 1820, troops finished the Military Road and a ferry began operation on the Tombigbee River near what Columbians today call the Old Highway 82 Bridge. Part Indian John Pitchlyn (also spelled Pytchlyn and Pitchlynn) was regularly seen along the river in those days, for he was an interpreter and a sub-agent for the Choctaw Nation. Pitchlyn had been in the area since around 1806.

The town of Columbus was incorporated in 1821, at that same time the first free public school in Mississippi was organized here. Franklin Academy opened its doors in Columbus on February 10, 1821, Shortly thereafter, Columbus became a port of call where the steamboat, Cotton Plant, docked in 1822.

When the new state of Mississippi abolished the Choctaw Tribal government in 1829, the western part of what is now Lowndes County was acquired from the Choctaws at the Treaty of Dancing Rabbit Creek. The terms of the treaty specified that the Choctaws leave Lowndes County in 1833, and thus more land was opened for white settlement.

The Greek Revival architectural style was soon to be full-blown in the South, for its appeal seemed to coincide with the arrival of settlers who came to claim Indian lands. The grand mansions were built as much for protection from the elements as for show, for the settlers soon learned that the hot Mississippi sun could be relentless, thus the need for porches —or porticoes, galleries, verandas, depending on which word seems appropriate for the house since they all mean practically the same— with tall ceilings to allow for breezes. The well-built houses, with shutters to keep out both sun and cold winter wind, were necessary for comfort. But there was a certain amount of pride involved in building ornate houses. After all, those who could afford the fine homes were justly proud of their affluence.

Generally, the Greek Revival houses arose between 1820 and 1860. In some circles the style is referred to simply as Southern architecture because it employs classical elements with a hint of the Georgian. The latter style was popular along the East Coast in the 1700s; it was followed by the Colonial architecture of 1750-1800. Some architectural historians say that "Southern Colonial," sometimes used in reference to the massive houses in Mississippi, is inappropriate because anything "colonial" must refer to the colonies, and the Deep South states were never colonies.

Columbus is known for a style called "Columbus Eclectic" because several prominent houses feature a combination of Greek Revival, Italianate, and Gothic styles. Also in Columbus, several Italianate homes were constructed in the late 1840s and 1850s. The Italianate was the last of the European "Revivals" in the South, though throughout the Southern region and the period of extensive construction, Greek Revival remained the favorite style.

The years from 1835 to the late 1850s were perhaps the most prosperous in the history of Columbus. Cotton production and sales were at an all-time high, and more furniture and decorative items for the grand homes came up the Tombigbee River on barges. The shipping route was often from Europe, to Mobile, to makeshift ports along the Tombigbee River. On occasion, some furnishings from France arrived in New Orleans, and pushed up the Mississippi River to Natchez, where wagons waited to bring them up what is now known as the Natchez Trace.

"Reflections" showcases the antebellum homes of Columbus in chronological order as they were built, beginning with the first and ending with those built just prior to the Civil War. You'll see that some are far more ornate than others, but the differences represent the lifestyles of the day. After the war, survival took precedence over grandeur, and the homes of another era were remnants in need of repair.

Today, as you will see on these pages, the homes of Columbus are once again as resplendent as the day there were built. Hats off to the dedicated preservationists who own and maintain these homes of history!

The Cedars c.1810
1305 Military Road

The Cedars, the oldest existing house in Columbus and Lowndes County, was built around 1810 on a hill overlooking the old Indian Trail, which was soon to be named Jackson's Military Road.

As the pioneer style of the day dictated, The Cedars was originally a one-room log house with a loft above. Though the early history of the house is somewhat vague, it was purchased in 1835 by Captain Edward Brett Randolph, a native Virginian, who also owned and operated the now extinct Goshen Plantation. According to local legend, Captain Randolph had ridden through this area enroute to his home in Virginia after the War of 1812. Perhaps he decided then to return to this lovely and lush land so perfect for farming.

He returned in the 1820s, bought and worked the Goshen land until 1830, when he freed his slaves before sending them to Liberia on a chartered ship. With no help to farm the land, Randolph moved nearer to town and bought The Cedars which, appropriately, remains in the family today. Randolph began transforming The Cedars from a log cabin to a home more appropriate to his station in life.

Edward Randolph was appointed Collector of Public Monies for Land Sales. Rumors abound that the industrious and educated gentleman planter found local banking facilities inadequate and unsatisfactory, so he stored much of the collected money in a secret place under the stairs at his home. The Cedars became a safe haven, of sorts, for public monies before the funds were sent on to Washington.

During the Civil War, Confederate States of America (CSA) General Nathan Bedford Forrest was a guest of the Randolphs, and so was Union General Benjamin Grierson, though not at the same time. Reports of the day indicated that the honorable General Grierson once returned to The Cedars a pair of mules that his troops had confiscated.

Today, Lt. Col. (ret.) and Mrs. Robert Hardy are the keepers of the homeplace, and they are proud to share their home's history with interested parties. The original rough hewn logs are covered with white siding, and sturdy columns support the veranda, which was added long ago. Spacious wings were also added to the side and rear of the house.

Inside, the warmth of rich wood is most appropriate to the home, with family heirlooms and antiques adding to the Cedars' historic significance. Of special interest is the exposed original log wall in the parlor.

The Cedars is on the National Register of Historic Places; it is located at 1305 Military Road.

Photo By Sylvia Higginbotham

Hope Cottage c.1820-1849
1315 Fourth Avenue North

What this rambling, one-story frame home lacks in documentation, it makes up for in charm. It is believed that the two middle rooms were built around 1820, with major additions made in 1849.

Now the home of David and Mona Sanders and family, Hope Cottage is a comfortable family home with many special attributes. The Greek Revival cottage-style home has spacious rooms and a front portico as well as a long, narrow portico on each side. The addition of an enclosed sun porch on a corner of the front came about much later, for it is not period-specific.

According to Mona Sanders, the addition made in 1849 can still be detected if one looks carefully. The 12-inch heart pine lumber used for construction is pegged; random-width pine floors remain in place today. Other clues to the age of Hope Cottage are the irregular door facings, jib windows, and a separate kitchen (now connected to the house).

Hope Cottage was once the home of a local jeweler who is said to have stored his jewels in the attic, though the current residents have searched sedulously for hidden jewelry to no avail.

Hope Cottage is located at 1315 Fourth Avenue North.

Hickory Sticks c.1820
1206 Seventh Street North

Hickory Sticks, c. 1820, is one of the oldest homes in Columbus. It was originally a log cabin, though today, as it peeks mysteriously through the tall trees and foliage, it appears to be a typical Greek Revival showplace. Indeed, Hickory Sticks has come a long way from its austere beginnings as a one and one-half story log cabin, with four rooms built in "dog trot" style. Dog trot features a long central hall with rooms opening off the hall. The house now faces Seventh Street, though at the time of its construction it faced what is now Lee Park.

Several additions and restorations were made by various owners, the first of which was sanctioned in the 1830s by the president of the first bank in Columbus, Andrew Weir. A stairway was added, then in the 1840s, considerable remodeling was done. At this time, the Greek facade was created, with the additions of columns and a veranda.

Years after serving as a residence of prominent families, Hickory Sticks was sold to General Stephen D. Lee, who later bequeathed the property to Blewett Lee. Blewett gave part of the property to the City of Columbus, thus the name Lee Park.

Later owners discovered the old log walls in the original rooms; they removed the plaster to leave the log walls exposed. Among previous owners were the Robert Ivy, Sr. family. Mrs. Fran Ivy continues to reside in Columbus where she writes a column for the **Commercial Dispatch**; her son, Robert, an architect/magazine editor, lives in New York City.

Hickory Sticks, perched regally on a hill at 1206 Seventh Street near Lee Park, is one of the most private homes in Columbus, for it is practically hidden from the street. Hickory Sticks is listed on the National Register of Historic Places.

Belmont c.1821
Neilson Road

Completed in 1822, Belmont is the earliest existing home in the countryside of Lowndes County. According to local legend, the homesite was selected during the War of 1812, when Captain William Walker Neilson rode through the area back to his Maryland home from New Orleans. Perhaps Captain Neilson and his friend, Captain Edward Brett Randolph, decided at this time to return to the area so rich in virgin timber, plentiful springs, gently rolling hills, and adjacent prairie land where bumper crops would surely grow.

Captain Neilson was a proud Irishman, born in Donegal, who arrived in Baltimore as a child. He made good his vow to return to Mississippi, and did so in 1820. Both Neilson and Randolph applied for land grants to build their houses, and both were awarded the grants once the Chickasaws had relinquished control of the land.

Belmont's beginnings were more modest than the home of today indicates, for the original structure had only two large rooms. In late 1821, when Capt. Neilson went "up North" to fetch his bride, he left a fellow Irishman in charge of completing the construction of Belmont. The newlyweds saw that the itinerant Irishman had gone elsewhere, leaving less industrious others in charge of the work. The young couple had to live in the smokehouse for a year while their home was finished.

Furniture, hardware, glassware and such came by overland coach from Philadelphia and Baltimore. White pillars were placed on the front to support the porch, though porch and pillars were later removed because one Neilson son had gout and required the healing powers of the sun.

Sarah Neilson died giving birth to her seventh child. Later, Neilson married Miss Louisa Abert Pinkney. They had four children, one of whom married Miss Eliza Lucy Irion in 1871. Miss Lucy, born in 1843, wrote a diary of the Civil War years called "Lucy's Journal."

Belmont is now the home of Doug and Leslie Webber and family. It is located on Neilson Road, off Wolfe Road, which is a few miles east of Columbus on Hwy. 12.

Detail of the porch ceiling.

Magnolia Hill c.1825
1106 Twelfth Street North

At the time of its construction —thought to be in the mid-1820s— Magnolia Hill was a two-room raised log cabin that faced Military Road. In the 1830s, a more formal structure was built around this cabin by Thomas C. McGee. McGee died in 1837, after which time his wife sold the home to the W.B. Winston family; he was a banker from Natchez who came to be the cashier for the bank in Columbus.

The Winstons added two Greek Revival wings to the house in the 1840s, and they added a large porch with a curved, canopy-style roof to the east and the south sides. William Winston died in 1850, though his wife Rebecca remained at Magnolia Hill throughout the Civil War. Her daughter, Maria, and son-in-law, Dr. Cornelius Hardy, inherited the home at Rebecca Winston's death. The house remained in the Hardy family until 1948.

Original floor boards, doors and some hand-blown "bottle-glass" window panes remain, along with the simple but elegant 1830s staircase. The J. Dudley Hutchinson family bought Magnolia Hill in 1948 and began to modernize the home, while preserving its original characteristics and charm.

Magnolia Hill

Current owners Dr. and Mrs. Terry Stubblefield purchased the home in 1999. It is the second home that they have restored in Columbus. Their interest in preservation and restoration have led them to an appreciation of the workmanship and craftsmanship found in historic homes. They spend much of their time conducting research and engaging in hands-on restoration techniques. They also enjoy collecting antiques appropriate to the age and style of the house.

Like many other antebellum homes in the South, Magnolia Hill is not without a story. Sometime in October 1862 and during the War Between the States, Mrs.Elizabeth Meriwether of Memphis came through Columbus on the way to Alabama. Her husband was a CSA officer; she had been banished from her home, and had with her everything she could carry in a mule-pulled wagon and still have room for two children and an old servant. She initially stayed at the hotel in Columbus but was advised to leave because the Yankees were at West Point and might have been heading to Columbus. She left for Tuscaloosa, got as far as Pickensville, Alabama, before she decided her family would be better off in Columbus. After all, she was expecting her third child, and cold weather was upon them. Someone told her that old Mrs. Winston sometimes took boarders, so she arrived at Magnolia Hill with plans to stay a few nights and ended up staying five months. She felt safe at Mrs. Winston's house.

On Christmas night 1862, after the children had received their Christmas gifts of tiny horns and were soundly sleeping by the fire, the baby came, thanks to the help and compassion of a black midwife. Elizabeth named her baby Lee, for General Robert E. Lee.

In the spring of 1863, she finally made it to Tuscaloosa, and after the war, the family returned to Memphis. Lee Meriwether, born at Magnolia Hill, became a world traveler and writer, and for all their lives, the Meriwether boys were ardent fans of General Lee, CSA President Jefferson Davis, and Columbus, Mississippi.

Magnolia Hill now uses its lovely rear entrance as its main entrance, which faces 1106 Twelfth Street North.

Magnolia Hill Parlor

Kidd's Tavern c.1826
Highway 12

The old place east of town known as Kidd's Tavern was built around 1826 by a Mr. Thomason, who used it as a tavern and stagecoach stop. The style, according to historic preservationist and Columbus architect Sam Kaye, AIA, is "Southern I Beam." Constructed of heart pine, the all-wood house has 10-foot ceilings and a porch extending across the front.

Originally, Kidd's Tavern had two rooms downstairs and two rooms upstairs; it was a typical dog-trot style with a wide center hall and rooms off each side. Today, it is much loved and appreciated by current owners, Tim and Janet Butler, who bought the house and three acres in 1994. Janet was an Andrews, a well-known old family name in Columbus and Lowndes County, and she has researched the history of her home.

She said that Mr. Thomason sold the place to the Kidd family around 1832. The Kidds continued to operate the tavern and stagecoach stop for a while. Duels and frontier-type lawlessness were apparent, for musket ball holes are still punched in the ceiling of one bedroom.

"Another rumor surrounds the Kidds and their time at the tavern," Janet Butler said "Supposedly, one of their daughters ran off with a controversial stagecoach driver, perhaps a man of a different race. She was disowned by her distraught family. It is believed that she was later buried on the property, though no grave marker has been found."

The Kidds owned the tavern until after the Civil War. In 1867, the mother of the Rev. Thomas B. Wood bought the house as a home for her family and her war-injured brother. The brother had traveled through the area as a soldier, and always wanted to return to this appealing land. Later, the Rev. Wood established Cumberland Presbyterian churches in the vicinity. He also used the place as a theological seminary, where he taught college students, and he used it as a circulating library.

The house remained in the Wood family from 1867 until the Butlers bought it. It is located about nine miles northeast of Columbus on Highway 12.

Cartney-Hunt House c.1828
408 Seventh Street South

The original part of the red-brick Cartney-Hunt House was built around 1828. Today it is something of a rarity among the Greek Revivals and Italianates that later sprang up around it. Cartney-Hunt, named for the land speculator James Cartney and the merchant Henry Hunt, who built the house, represents a Federal-style architecture that came west with the early settlers of the region.

New owners enlarged the home in 1846 by adding a two-story wing and a center hall. Later, Victorian design elements were added, which remained until the house fell into disrepair, then was salvaged when concerned local citizens, headed by Hunter Gholson, purchased it and hired local architect Sam Kaye to restore the house to its 1846 heyday. In 1983, the Cartney-Hunt House won a restoration award and designation as an historic property.

The Cartney-Hunt, located at 408 Seventh Street S., is the home of Kirk and Vicki Hardy and family.

The house is listed on the National Register of Historic Places.

Photo By Sylvia Higginbotham

The Proffitt Home c.1826-1846
571 Ridge Road

The Proffitt Home was originally a one-story frame house located in town behind the old Bell Tavern, though now it's resting comfortably in a country haven among tall pines and magnolias. It is believed that this structure served as the first post office in Columbus, since the U.S. Mail was sent from and received at a place of the same description. Gideon Lincecum was the first postmaster.

This historically significant house was also once the residence of Dr. William Lowndes Lipscomb and his new bride. Dr. Lipscomb was a prominent physician in the late 1800s, and he was a writer. His early history of Columbus is still widely used today.

The house --much smaller then-- has been moved twice, in 1846 and again in 1973. For the last move, the house was cut in half and moved in two sections. Before it was bought and moved by Bob and Elizabeth Proffitt, the house served as a Sunday School classroom site for First United Methodist Church. It had been scheduled for demolition when the Proffitts purchased it. Today, it's a lovely family home.

Of particular interest is the piano in the parlor of the Proffitt home. It once belonged to Colonel George Hampton Young, who built Waverley. Elizabeth Proffitt is Young's great, great granddaughter. The Proffitt Home is located at 571 Ridge Road.

The Post House c.1828
Highway 12

The historic home of the Harry Sanders family was built in the late 1820s, and in its early life, it served briefly as a post house —or depot.   People traveling on the overland stage could buy tickets for their journey there, or stop for a rest or an overnight.

Clues to the early use of this interesting structure include three front doors. One led to what was likely a ticket office, where a stairway led to what may have been a bunk room for drivers and/or passengers. The Post House is a big, sturdy, no-frills house built for utility rather than show. The house has a two-story front, with a sloping, lean-to back.

Amazingly, the Post House has had few owners, and it has not been drastically altered during various add-ons. The original brick kitchen still serves the meals. A Mr. McGowan from Texas was the original owner; he sold it to the Waring family. For many years, the place was known as the Waring Country Place. It is still connected to the Warings, for Harry Sanders' paternal grandmother was a Waring.

The Post House is located a few miles northeast of Columbus on Highway 12.

Liberty Hall Foyer

Liberty Hall c.1832
Armstrong Road

By 1831, Columbus had grown in population to around 500, which made the area even more attractive to planters who came from the Carolinas seeking new cotton land and a good quality of life for their families. Among those early residents of Lowndes County were the William Ervin family from Sumter, South Carolina. Ervin, who had been a state senator in South Carolina, had heard of the vast tracts of Indian land opened for settlement, so he headed west from the Carolinas, arrived in east Mississippi, and bought 4000 acres of virgin land west of Columbus for about $1.25 an acre.

His son, William Ethelbert Ervin, soon built a big, rambling home for his family. He chose to build on the plantation site east of the new town rather than in the town, about seven miles away. The two-story frame house was completed in 1832 and named Liberty Hall.

Liberty Hall is one of the few homes in Lowndes County known to be still in the family of the original builder, which is a fact that adds the utmost authenticity to the historic property. The W.S. "Monk" Fowler family owns Liberty Hall today, and they continue the family traditions established so long ago.

Mrs. Sarah Fowler, great-great-granddaughter of William Ethelbert Ervin, tells true and treasured stories of the old family place and the interesting people who lived there, including her late mother —known by the family as "Hottie"— and her two aunts who lived there with the Fowlers until the elderly aunts died. They were Aunts Penelope and Caro; Aunt Caro was also known by the family as Barbo.

Liberty Hall

The Fowler family still gathers at Liberty Hall for Sunday dinner, as they've always done. "Sunday dinner" in these parts means the meal served after the morning church service; it is usually on the table by early afternoon. Sarah regales the children with stories about the family and Liberty Hall, surely some of the same stories she heard as a child.

"Aunt Caro —Barbo to us— was a wonderful storyteller. She never married, and she delighted in telling stories to the children of the family. She would continue them from one Sunday to the next. Remember, these were the days before television, so we couldn't wait 'til the next Sunday to hear the rest of the story. Barbo's stories were our much-anticipated entertainment," recalls Sarah.

She also tells her own grandchildren about the ancestors whose paintings hang on the walls of Liberty Hall, among them Sarah's great-great-great grandparents. And then there's the artist who came to Liberty Hall in the late 1850s to paint oil murals of French country scenes. He put them on the wooden panels high on the walls of the dining room. But the ones he started on the dining-room hall are still as unfinished as they were at the outbreak of the Civil War, when the artist returned to South Carolina to join a regiment from his state.

Sarah also tells the grandchildren about their grandfather, the late Monk Fowler, a Navy pilot who was called "King of the Sub Killers" in articles, because he sank more enemy submarines in World War II than any other Navy pilot. Commander Fowler, a decorated war hero, flew torpedo bombers off a carrier.

Another amazing story is that Liberty Hall is thought to be the world's first antebellum mobile home. Here's how Sarah tells the story...

"During the hard times around the 1920s, my grandmother was a widow and had begun supplementing her income through the sale of gravel dug on the place. The people who were excavating the gravel got closer to the house, and soon discovered a wealth of gravel under the house. They asked Grandmother if they could move her house, and she said 'no'. Because, she said, her 'Great grandmother had brought the boxwoods and other landscaping shrubs all the way from South Carolina! And there was the school house, smoke house, and other buildings that would have to be moved, too. It was just impossible,' Grandmother said.

"Well, as it happened, a cyclone hit in 1921, and destroyed the landscaping and the out-buildings. Grandmother decided that the cyclone was a 'sign' from above, so she let them move the house.

"They used one mule and a wench, and inched the house along on rollers, so slowly, nobody realized it was being moved. There was no indoor plumbing or electricity to worry about disturbing, so the family continued to live in the house for the many months it took to move it a short distance, about a quarter mile. "My aunts always laughed and said they lived in the first antebellum mobile home!"

When Liberty Hall was built, there were two rooms downstairs and two rooms upstairs, with a detached kitchen. To accommodate a growing family in the 1840s, Ervin and other family members added two bedrooms downstairs, two upstairs, a back hall, back stairs, dining room hall, and a porch.

Liberty Hall is a comfortable, white frame planter's home with the facade dominated by a central pediment supported by a double set of square columns. The interior is not adorned with ornate plaster molding; it is, rather, a house that is casual except for the formal parlor, and the kind of place one hopes will never change. Nine family portraits, ranging from Mrs. Fowler's great-great-great-great grandmother to her children, emphasize the family's permanence in the home since 1832.

The house sits on a slight incline, surrounded by tall pines and hardwood trees, facing the iron-fenced family burial plot just to the far right of the front of the house. Some of the family members resting in peace at Liberty Hall were born in the 1780s. Confirming the family's continuity, a visitor can also see the grave of Barbo, the story teller, Dr. Francis Ervin, a Civil War surgeon, and Monk Fowler. A third century of tributes begins with a memorial stone to the Fowlers' daughter, Fran Fowler Hazard.

Listed on the National Register of Historic Places, Liberty Hall is about six miles east of Columbus off Armstrong Road.

Liberty Hall Dining Room

Pratt Thomas Home c.1833
519 Second Street South

Rumor has it that the Pratt Thomas Home is a favorite of architectural students who come into Columbus to study the treasures of antebellum architecture. Perhaps it's the "welcoming arms" stairway, or maybe it's the symmetry and proportion of this uniquely designed house that garners so much attention. The recessed gallery is flanked by two wings, with round, fluted, Ionic columns sitting under the hipped roof and cupola.

The style is raised cottage, with a floor plan that includes a cross hall with double parlors behind the hall. Black marble mantels are original to this truly elegant home. Few families have owned the home since its construction. The builder, Adolphus B. Weir, a government agent in Indian affairs, sold his home to Colonel William C. Richards in 1870. It remained in the Richards family for more than one hundred years. Richards' granddaughter was Mrs. Pratt Thomas. The home is now owned by Thomas descendants.

The Pratt Thomas Home is located at 519 Second Street South, directly across from Riverview. It is listed on the National Register of Historic Places.

The Fort House c.1833
510 Seventh Street North

Because of its location on the corner of Seventh Street and Fifth Avenue North, the Fort House is one of the most visible houses in Columbus. It is hard to miss, for it sits on a hill, watching over the nearby town, reminding all who pass that indeed, this is architectural perfection at its best. Once known as Themerlaine, the house was purchased by the Don DePriest family in the late 1980s and a major restoration was soon underway. If you want to see an historic property that has been perfectly and painstakingly restored, this is it.

Research indicated that the home had originally been referred to as the Elias Fort House or the Martha Fort House, so the new owners decided to reinstate the original family name. The earliest date given to the Fort House prior to the restoration project had been 1844. However, clues in the house's architectural structure and in courthouse records led to further exploration and research, which indicated that the house had been standing in 1833.

Martha Williams Battle Fort owned the home from at least 1833 to 1877. Her first husband was Elias B. Fort, whom she met and married in Nash County, North Carolina. The Fort family came to Mississippi in a carriage leading a caravan, sometime in the 1820s. They came through Tuscaloosa, Alabama, and visited her brother, Alfred Battle, whose home, the Battle-Friedman House, is today a tourist attraction in Tuscaloosa.

In 1830, Elias Fort died on his plantation one mile over the Alabama State line from Lowndes County, Mississippi.

The widow Fort married Elisha Sharp in 1837, but divorced him in 1840. She and her children took back the Fort name, and shortly thereafter, their home was the site of parties and social gatherings. It is believed that in the mid-1840s, major architectural features were added, among them the Greek Revival features and the double porticoes and cross hall, which remain distinct architectural features.

The Fort House once again is in its prime. More than twenty rooms and 9,700 square feet create a sense of space rivaled only by the home's sense of place in the history of Columbus. The interior is period perfect, in colors, wallpaper, furniture and art.

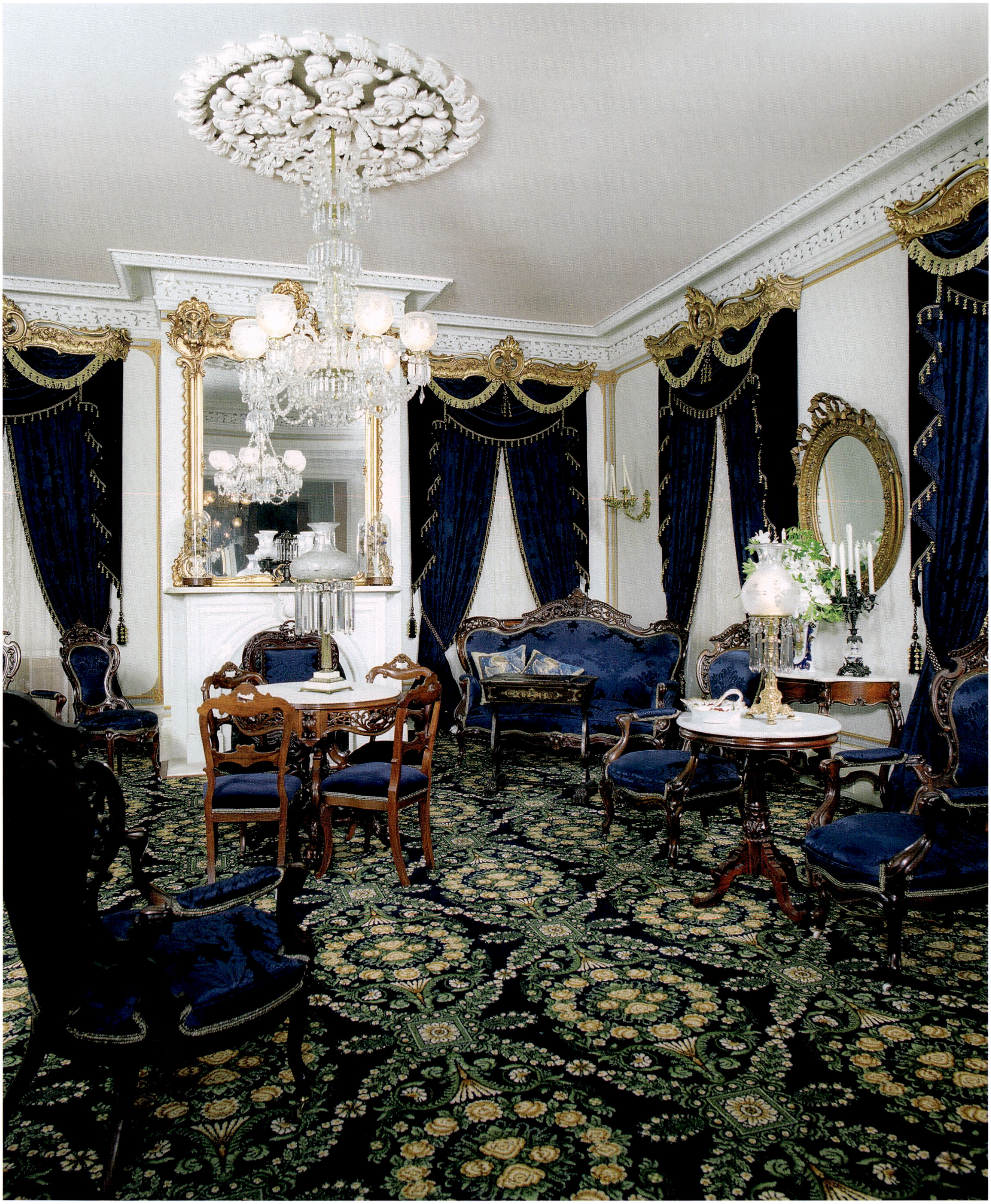

The Fort House Blue Parlor

The Fort House

The Fort House Parlor

Cosmetic and structural work gave the grand old house a new lease on life, including new plaster reproduction, new marbleizing and woodgraining, and more. Original material was used whenever possible, as in the window panes. Those remaining were salvaged after the sash was removed, dipped, stripped, and primed. The original foundation bricks were also removed, then re-used with new mortar. More than 13,000 bricks, laid in a herringbone pattern, grace the ground floor, a place much appreciated by the active DePriest family.

To augment and secure the foundation, load-bearing walls were reinforced with concrete and steel footing. A new copper roof was added, and the Fort House should be set for another hundred years or so.

Owners Don and Sandra DePriest exercised great care in renovating their home. For example, the library features period reproduction Stark carpet, reproduced as it would have been made in 18-inch wide looms. The wallpaper is custom Zuber paper, the color and style from the 1830-1850 period.

Woodgraining has been meticulously applied throughout; marbleizing appears to be the original Egyptian black marble; plaster cornice was repaired throughout, and every aspect of this house that needed refurbishing received expert attention.

Enter the foyer; on each side find parlors where important antique furniture includes parlor furniture by John Henry Belter, Rosalie pattern, and a three-piece French Empire salon set, 19th century. There's also a Belter Rococo Revival carved mahogany mirror door credenza, a Rococo Revival tester bed attributed to Francois Seignoret; two bookcases by Prudent Mallard, and other rare pieces.

The Fort House, listed on the National Register of Historic Places, sits at 510 Seventh Street North.

Lincoln Home c.1833
714 Third Avenue South

The Lincoln Home is one of the charming old places that has always been taken for granted. Since the early days, it has quietly gone about the business of maintaining a bird's eye view of Columbus. It sits two blocks south of Main Street, and just west of the Mississippi University for Women campus.

The old Lincoln place was home to the Lincoln family for about 135 years. The original three-room house was built around 1833 by David Love, the father of Amzi Love, to be used as a carriage/guest house. Love's primary residence was on Seventh Street South, adjoining the carriage house. David Love sold the property to Barney B. Lincoln in the early 1840s, and Lincoln began re-construction. The Lincoln's added rooms on the east side, a porch, and gables. The kitchen was originally in the basement, along with the carriage house and stable. The style today is a "raised cottage" that features blue and red Venetian side lights around the front door. The Lincoln Home has a welcoming front porch that beckons all who enter.

Lincoln's son Cicero, who was two years old when the family moved into the house, served in the Civil War and the Spanish American War. He was also a self-taught lawyer who read law books and passed the bar exam in 1900. C.L. Lincoln was elected mayor of Columbus in 1901; he had previously served as circuit clerk, sheriff, and chancery clerk. He died in 1938 at the age of 94. His daughter, Miss Sue Mae Lincoln, continued to live in the home throughout her life. One of her brothers, Lonnie Lincoln, lived there as well.

Owners Sidney and Brenda Caradine, who also own the Amzi Love Bed & Breakfast Home next door, have made considerable improvements to the Lincoln Home, now a popular bed-and- breakfast inn, too. They added brick floors downstairs in the original basement, along with insulation, new wiring and plumbing. During the renovation, the Caradines found original artifacts from the home's early days.

The Lincoln Home restoration project won a Restoration Heritage Award from the Mississippi Heritage Trust; it was one of only 14 awards bestowed in 1999.

The home is located at 714 Third Avenue South.

Franklin Square c.1835
423 Third Avenue North

It is hard to miss this red brick mansion, for it sits on a busy corner of Hwy. 45 and Third Avenue North, near downtown. Since the mid-1830s, Franklin Square has been perched on a slight incline to the south of a deep ravine and across the street from the state's first free elementary school, Franklin Academy.

One of the earliest brick houses in Columbus, the house underwent an expansion when Sidney Franklin bought it in 1870. He added the south facade, and made minor interior changes. Double columns support the pediment, with identical doors on both stories overlooking an old brick fence. Decorative railings surround two balconies.

Pioneer builder and contractor Neill Bartee was commissioned by Paschal B. Wade to build the house. Franklin Square is still in the Franklin family, with the William Rosamond family, the sixth generation, now in residence.

Located at 423 Third Avenue North, Franklin Square remains one of the most visible historic homes in Columbus.

Rosewood Manor c.1835
719 Seventh Avenue North

More than three thousand boxwoods, a rose garden, an herb garden, a cutting garden, and massive old trees surround the aptly named Rosewood Manor, which reigns over four and a half acres of landscaped lawn. A recent addition to the 1835 house and garden is a small chapel thought to be about 100 years old, with a past life as a plantation chapel. The chapel is situated near the gazebo. The beautiful little chapel contains original stained-glass windows and woodwork, including pews and an altar rail. Homeowners Grayce and Dewitt Hicks use the chapel for private meditation, and for events that require limited seating, such as small weddings and the christening of their youngest grandchild.

Built by planter Richard Sykes, the stately Rosewood Manor was built to last. It boasts brick walls that are three-bricks thick, now painted white. The Greek Revival facade with a Federal influence features a two-story portico supported by two giant Doric columns, with a balcony over the entrance.

Original heart-pine flooring sets off the neoclassical interior and the fine antiques and heirlooms. The four-over-four style features four rooms on each floor, with each room opening off a central hall. A circular carriage drive was paved with bricks in a herringbone pattern; the drive is still in use today.

Rosewood Manor

Rosewood Manor Garden

Over the years, Rosewood Manor has been the home of many prominent Columbus families, among them Middleton Wooten, whose wife was the granddaughter of two governors; Governor James L. Alcorn of Mississippi and Governor Rector of Arkansas. Also, the house was called home by Mrs. Hezekiah Leigh, whose husband, the Rev. Hezekiah Leigh, was one of the founders of Randolph Macon College. The home has been called Birdhaven, Wooten Manor, Fairleigh Manor, and Maydrew Manor, though Rosewood Manor seems most appropriate.

Rosewood Manor, listed on the National Register of Historic Places, is a few blocks from downtown at 719 Seventh Avenue North. Tours are available year 'round.

Homewood c.1836
800 Second Street South

The striking, Greek Revival-style Homewood was built by the merchant W.M. Cozart around 1836. Later, for about one hundred years, it was known simply as the Billups-Cox home on Main Street. Yes, Homewood's presence graced Main Street until 1975, when it was cut in half and moved to its present location. Indeed, the grand old mansion created much controversy back in the 1970s when it was a house without a home.

The site on Main Street was purchased by the First Columbus National Bank, now AmSouth, which was planning a new building on that corner. When the existing structure could not be incorporated into the bank's design, much discussion ensued concerning its future. It was in danger of demolition, but bank owners, Historic Columbus —the promotion arm of the Columbus Pilgrimage— a local developer and local government gave it a new lease on life and a new address. What a sight it must have been: one half of a big frame house inching its way south down 7th Street to the railway tracks, then traveling the tracks to 2nd Street. Unfortunately, during the move, one side collapsed and had to be re-built; it was the side that had lost the support of the brick fireplace.

Today, Homewood's residents, the Wil Colom family, continues to enjoy the meticulous attention to detail that occurred during the restoration. Classic and Romantic Revival influences are evident at Homewood. The pillars on the portico were heightened during the after-move reconstruction. Such design elements as richly colored etched glass in the transom and sidelights, crystal chandeliers, and brass door hardware remain.

There were those who said the mansion could not be moved. Luckily for others who worked so diligently to save this outstanding example of Southern-style architecture, it is now fitter and finer than ever.

Homewood is located at 800 Second Street South.

Temple Heights Foyer

Temple Heights c.1837
515 Ninth Street North

Known as one of the state's best examples of period restorations, this imposing house on a hill is Greek Revival on the outside, though the interior style is Federal. The builder of this Grecian-like temple, Richard T. Brownrigg, came to Columbus from Edenton, North Carolina, to seek his fortune "to the west." Indeed he did achieve success as a cotton planter.

The house Brownrigg built in Mississippi bears a strong resemblance to his wife's family home, Mulberry Hill, on the Albemarle Sound in North Carolina. After General Brownrigg's death in 1846, Thomas Harris purchased Temple Heights in 1847 at the sale price of $3,600. Other owners were the Fontaine family, and the Kennebrews, from 1887 to 1965. Former resident, Miss Jane Fontaine, was one of the Decoration Day ladies who inspired the poem "The Blue and the Gray," and subsequently Memorial Day.

Columbus businessman Kirk Egger in 1965 purchased the house from the Kinnebrews to save it, and it was he who sold it to current owners, Carl and Dixie Butler.

"Kirk Egger wanted the house to be restored, and he wouldn't sell it to anyone who wouldn't restore it. I came here in the summer of 1965 to coach swimming. I'd always been interested in historic properties, and knew about Temple Heights but was told it was uninhabitable. It was in terrible shape, visually; it had not been painted in 40 years. But we kept looking at it and thinking about it," explained Carl Butler.

"After Dixie and I got engaged, we decided we wanted this house and made the commitment to restore it, if Mr. Egger would sell it to us. Our friends Bill Lee Sanders, Virginia Hooper and Ed Keaton wrote to Kirk Egger saying that 'the young couple' would be good ones to buy and restore the house," added Butler.

"Their recommendation worked. He agreed to let us buy it, and since we were both in graduate school in Nashville —Dixie at Peabody; I was at Vanderbilt— he let us pay $1,000 down and arranged it so that we didn't have to pay more until after grad school," said Butler. Both Carl and Dixie Butler are educators whose love of history is evident in their home.

Temple Heights Foyer

A Temple Heights Bedroom

Over the years, the Butlers have acquired an important collection of Parian porcelain, along with a fine collection of period antiques and decorative arts. Their advice to anyone interested in buying and restoring an historic property is to conduct major research. They say to start at the local public library. Study the time period, the architecture, and the decorative arts. Then contact the Department of Archives and History in your state; ask for information. Dixie suggests studying the paintings of the era. The key, they agree, is extensive and continuing research.

Temple Heights is a Mississippi Landmark, on the Historic American Building Survey, and it is listed on the National Register of Historic Places. The grand old Greek Revival sits on a hill at 515 Ninth Street North.

Corner Cottage c.1837
304 Fourth Avenue South

The pleasant pale yellow two-story frame house on Fourth Avenue South was built around 1837 by Dr. Aurelius N. Jones, a local physician and druggist, and later a state representative. Dr. Jones initiated the building of the Greek Revival home Leighcrest several years later, though the house on the corner represents the transition from late Federal to Greek Revival. It began as a one room dwelling, with other rooms added later.

The J.M. Symons family and descendants owned the cottage-style house until 1937; they sold it to Mrs. Llewellyn Hatchett. It was bought by the Frank Herndons around 1938; he was a professor at Mississippi University for Women. The Herndons gave it the name "Corner Cottage."

A concealed staircase —called "hidden stair" because it was hidden by a closet door— is an unusual feature of this house. The staircase is very narrow, too narrow to transport heavy furniture to the second floor; consequently some furniture had to be hoisted for entry through the second story windows. There are six fireplaces and mantels; five bedrooms downstairs; and two bedrooms are upstairs.

Mrs. Legrande Sullivan began major restoration when she became the owner in the mid-1980s. For period accuracy, she consulted with the Mississippi Department of Archives and History. Legrande says that if you want a house to be correctly restored, you must make the effort and consult with experts. She adds that restoration is not easy, and once you start, there's no stopping. During restoration, they found two original windows hidden behind plaster, and they found a windowpane with a woman's name and date etched on it.

Today, the Corner Cottage is the residence of Mike and Cindy Sullivan Reese. Listed on the National Register of Historic Places, it is at 304 Fourth Avenue South.

Twelve Gables c.1838
220 Third Street South

This Columbus landmark is a local favorite as well as one of the state's most historically significant structures. The historic significance comes from the fact that, in 1866, a group of Columbus women met in this home to plan a way to honor the Confederate soldiers interred at the local cemetery. The simple gesture of placing flowers on the graves of the dearly departed at Decoration Day evolved into the nation's Memorial Day observance, for the gracious ladies also placed flowers on the graves of Union soldiers.

The generous and kindly deed was told and re-told until mention of it appeared in the *New York Tribune*. One reader, a young barrister named Francis Miles Finch, was so moved by the act of kindness that he wrote the poem, "The Blue and the Gray," excerpted here.

Twelve Gables was the home of the John Morton family for four generations. Today, it is the home of Ray and Trudy Gildea. It is furnished in fine antiques and heirloom pieces along with an important family art collection. Over the years, no major structural changes have occurred. The original kitchen was in the basement, though it was moved upstairs around the turn of the century.

Twelve Gables is a one and one-half story gable roof Greek Revival style frame residence with a full balustraded portico. Paneled square columns and rusticated wooden siding were designed to resemble ashlar stone. Updates include cosmetic design work, reinforcement of the stairway, a glass enclosed back porch and an open, roofed porch which overlooks the well planned and manicured lawn.

Here's an interesting bit of irony concerning Twelve Gables: the author of the 1866 poem about the ladies who first met in this house helped to found Cornell University in Ithaca, New York. Owners Ray and Trudy Gildea are both graduates of Cornell.

Twelve Gables is listed on the National Register of Historic Places. It is located at 220 Third Street South.

Detail of Statues in
Friendship Cemetery

The Blue and the Gray
By F. M. Finch (Excerpt)

From the silence of sorrowful hours
The desolate mourners go,
Lovingly laden with flowers
Alike for the friend and the foe;
Under the sod and the dew,
Waiting the Judgment Day;
Under the roses, the Blue
Under the lilies, the Gray.

So with an equal splendor
The morning sun rays fall,
With a touch impartially tender,
On the blossoms blooming for all;
Under the sod and the dew,
Waiting the Judgment Day;
Wet with the rain, the Blue;
Wet with the rain, the Gray.

No more shall the war cry sever,
Or the winding rivers be red;
They banish our anger forever
When they laurel the graves of our dead!
Under the sod and the dew,
Waiting the Judgment Day;
Love and tears for the Blue,
Tears and love for the Gray.

Lehmquen c.1838
613 Second Street South

Attorney George Clayton and his brothers-in-law made a mark on Columbus. First, Clayton and his wife came from Athens, Georgia, and built the home now known as Lehmquen. A few years later, Mrs. Clayton's brothers arrived and built homes nearby, White Arches and Whitehall. Though the brothers' homes were mansions, the Claytons wanted a comfortable town house for their growing family. Lehmquen is somewhat similar in design to another Columbus home built at the same time, Twelve Gables.

The one and one-half story house features Doric columns, corner block millwork, and two dormers with double windows. The front door, with its transom and sidelights, leads into a center hallway and a flying-wing staircase. Still in place are the original silver door knobs and keyhole covers.

At the time it was built, the house covered a city block, with dependencies in the rear. This Greek Revival raised cottage is important to Columbus history, for it later became the residence of Mrs. Augusta Murdock Sykes, who was believed to be the first woman to decorate the graves of Union soldiers at Friendship Cemetery.

Some of Mrs. Sykes' personal effects remain in the home, which is still owned by Sykes descendants, the Robert Ivy, Jr. family. Lehmquen, at 613 Second Street South, is listed on the National Register of Historic Places.

Aldan Hall c.1839
901 Seventh Avenue North

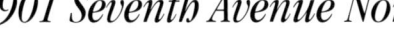

The Greek Revival home on Seventh Avenue North was built by John Topp, one of the first trustees of the Columbus Female Institute. The unpretentious townhouse of four rooms with a center stair hall was purchased in 1854 by James Sykes, a prominent early Columbian. The home was enlarged by the addition of a Federal-style portico with two octagonal fluted columns and a west wing. The staircase was also moved to the new side hall. The house was then in the shape of an "L," with the carriage house being built in a reverse "L." Subsequent additions increased the size and comfort of the home.

In 1982, Wayne and Betty Bryan became aware of the house which had been neglected for many years. After being assured by a knowledgeable relative that the house was basically sound, they bought the property and began extensive restoration. As lifelong residents of Columbus, the Bryans had loved the town's graceful old homes and could not bear to see this one abandoned.

During the lengthy restoration process, the Bryans found a trap door in the front hall that led to the basement. They also discovered that the transom and side lights around the front doors upstairs and down were designed to be removed during the summer for "air conditioning." It is believed that a walnut newell post on a staircase is the signature of architect/builder James Lull.

Under a concrete patio, the Bryans discovered a planter in the form of a magnetic compass. The planter brings great joy to all in the Spring. As each inhabitant adds to a home, the Bryans have added an arbor, terraced gardens, and an outdoor living area.

Aldan Hall, named for the two Bryan sons, is located at 901 Seventh Avenue North.

Worrell-Waggoner Home c.1840
405 Fourth Street South

It was 1840 when Kentuckian William Worrell bought this prime property from Richard Barry for $250. Worrell was a carpenter, a land speculator, father of 12, and later a city alderman who gave extra attention to detail to the house he built. Carved trim is abundant and most unusual. Religious crosses adorn the hand-carved columns on the front porch.

Other local names associated with the house are William Worrell's son John Worrell, Thomas Casey, the Cady family, who rented the house, and more. The late banker Davis Patty was born in this house when his parents were tenants. Willie Sims purchased the place in the 1940s, and the Sims estate sold to current owners Spencer and Mary Helen Waggoner in 1981. Today, it's a home much cherished by the Waggoner family.

The original dog-trot style that has evolved into eclectic style has 14-foot ceilings, with four rooms boasting a hall in the middle, and a porch on the front. At one time, the out buildings were enclosed and attached to the back of the house, though when Willie Sims bought the place in the 1940s, he tore down the uneven attachments to create a kitchen, breakfast, bath and utility.

The Worrell-Waggoner house sits comfortably among lovely old trees at 405 Fourth Street South.

The Barry House c.1840
506 Fourth Street South

Columbus is not short on houses associated with prominent politicians, and the Barry House is certainly one of those. It has been said that the house with definite Italianate styling and Gothic influences was "probably" built by Dr. William Topp, who later built the Italianate Rosedale. The Barry House, which was remodeled in the late 1800s, originally boasted a turret.

Known for its fine millwork, the two-story house features the original cypress beams and heart-pine flooring. Current owners Carol and Nancy Carpenter were enthralled with the beautiful, original molding, but quickly discovered that a section was missing. Later, they found the missing molding under the house. Nancy says that she sometimes sits and looks at the pocket doors, and thinks about the important political decisions that may have been made behind those closed doors.

In 1857, William S. Barry bought the ornate, two-story Italianate, and by that time, he had already built a political career for himself. Barry was a graduate of Yale Law School who became Speaker of the House of Representatives of Mississippi and he presided over the 1860 Mississippi Secession Convention. He was a delegate to the Confederate Congress in Montgomery, Alabama. He also owned plantations in Oktibbeha and Sunflower counties.

Surprisingly for someone who graduated Yale Law, Barry was an ardent secessionist. He presided over Mississippi's Secession Convention, which in turn sent him to the Provisional Congress. During the Civil War, he was the colonel of the 35th Mississippi Infantry; he was captured and paroled at Vicksburg; shot through the lung at Altoona, and captured the same day Lee surrendered at Appomattox. After the war, Barry practiced law in Columbus until his death in 1868.

The Barry House, located at 506 Fourth Street South, is listed on the National Register of Historic Places.

Photo By Sylvia Higginbotham

Max Andrews Home c.1840
403 Ninth Street South

The house now known as the Max Andrews has enjoyed previous service as a school and a stage coach inn. As the latter, it was once quite famous for "good fried chicken and clean beds," obvious perks for overland stage travelers.

Built around 1840 of board and batten construction, the sprawling, one-story cottage-style house was enlarged into an "H" shape by Green T. Hill, owner of the stage coach line. Hill was a prominent Columbus businessman whose wife was one of the Decoration Day ladies.

In 1948, Max and Cile Andrews bought the house for their family and for Cile to use as a kindergarten. The Andrews children and those enrolled in the school loved the old gazebo, which is still on the property today.

Fran Andrews Brown and her husband, Richard, acquired the Max Andrews Home in 1986. They enjoy it as a family home and as a popular B&B. The house is furnished with Empire and Victorian pieces, as well as family heirlooms.

The Max Andrews Home is located at 403 Ninth Street South.

Leighcrest c.1840
824 Seventh Street North

The Greek Revival Leighcrest is thought to have been the first local house designed by architect/ builder James Lull, who came to Columbus from Vermont. The house has been in the Leigh family since the mid-1800s; it is now the home of Frank and Martha Leigh. Martha Leigh said that Leighcrest may have been Lull's "spec house" in Columbus. Perhaps Dr. Aurelius N. Jones of Corner Cottage had the house built in 1841, though the title was in his wife's name, Cordelia A. Jones. Later owners were James O.Banks (1853 to 1865), William W. Whitfield (1865 to 1872), and Thomas W. Yates (1872 to 1876). James Sykes purchased it on December 29, 1876, and on the same day transferred ownership to Captain Frank M. Leigh.

Leighcrest has been occupied by Leighs since 1876, when Captain Leigh bought it . His family had lived across the street at what is now Rosewood Manor since 1853, when Mary Jane Crump Leigh, widow of Hezekiah G. Leigh, and her six children came from Virginia. She purchased Rosewood Manor from her cousin, Richard Sykes, and lived there until her death in 1883.

Leighcrest was originally part of a 1,000 acre estate, running between Bluecutt Road and Leigh Mall. Today Leigh Mall covers what was once the Leighs' dairy farm.

The current Leighs inherited the house in 1974; they began restoration in 1979, with their goal to restore their home to its original splendor. The house was structurally sound, but they replaced columns and porches, and had interior cosmetic work done.

This fine frame home has columns that reach up two stories. From its pristine location on a slight knoll, Leighcrest appears to be much the same as it was in the 1840s.

The gardens, too, recall an earlier time, for they are natural gardens where chemicals are banned. The Leigh's daughter Martha, who was an avid gardener, planted about 90 varieties of old-fashioned plants, including hollyhocks, delphiniums, yellow jasmine, iris, daffodils, magnolia fuscata, and more. In restoring the antebellum gardens, Martha determined the shapes of original beds by probing with a metal rod. The original bricks were excavated and re-laid in the patterns established more than one hundred years ago.

Leighcrest's lovely gardens are one of the few remaining examples of typical old Southern gardens laid out in a "parterre" arrangement. Steps lead to the terraced grounds, where walkways wind through the haven.

The garden serves as a memorial to Martha Leigh, Jr., who perhaps believed that..."A gardener plants for himself and those who come later."

Leighcrest is located at 824 Seventh Street North.

Harrison-Imes House c.1840
419 Ninth Street North

Since it was built, this historically significant house has been associated with local heroes who bear the names Blewett, Harrison, and Lee. Though there are conflicting reports concerning who actually built the house in the early 1840s, it appears that James T. Harrison bought the property in 1839; then Major James Garton Blewett had the home built for his daughter Regina and her husband, James Harrison. In 1856, Harrison added surrounding property to his holdings.

Major Blewett settled his family in Columbus in 1835. He quickly became a leader known for intelligence and wisdom. Blewett grew weary of a toll ferry on the Luxapalila, the narrow river that separated him from his plantations, so he petitioned the county to build a bridge and make it free to all local citizens. The strong, lattice-covered bridge officially opened in 1837, and he had quicker access to his land. Within a few years, Blewett began construction of his grand Italianate home on Seventh Street North, now known as The Lee Home.

Regina Blewett Harrison and her family prospered at their Ninth Street/Military Road home. The eclectic style of the Harrison-Imes is seen in Federal influences, though the symmetry of Greek Revival with Gothic traces is prominent, and the Italianate is noted in the masonry, ironwork, and chimneys.

Regina's husband, James, an attorney, was soon enough a leader among the state's barristers, and was later chosen by the state legislature to serve as Jefferson Davis's chief defense lawyer in his treason trial, should the trial materialize.

The Harrisons' daughter, also named Regina, married South Carolinian Stephen D. Lee in 1864, who was by then a general in the army of the Confederate States of America. Their wedding, at the Harrisons home, was a rare social occasion in the dark years of the Civil War. After the war, General S.D. Lee returned to Columbus and later became the first president of Mississippi State University, which opened in 1880.

The Harrisons son, James T., Jr., was also a prominent attorney and politician who later served the state as lieutenant governor from 1900 until 1904.

The Harrison family kept the house on Military Road until 1905, though Major Blewett left them his more opulent home on Seventh Street at his death in 1871. The S.D. Lees moved to their inherited home when Lee left his position at the Starkville college.

Today, the Harrison-Imes Home has undergone a major restoration and is the residence of entrepreneur Frank Imes. It is furnished in exquisite period antiques, mostly Continental. Imes is a noted collector of fine antiques and *objets d'art*. His home faces Military Road, at 419 Ninth Street North.

Harrison-Imes Dining Room

Arbor House c.1841
518 College Street

The pleasant, pastel green Italianate townhouse now known as Arbor House is indeed a house in town, for it is located one block off Main Street in downtown Columbus. It is believed that the house was built in two stages: first in 1841 and in 1854, or perhaps later. Even more construction continued well into the 1870s.

Arbor House has had many names over the years, and many incarnations. First a two-room cottage built by Benjamin Toomer, it was purchased by Colonel William Cady in 1841. Colonel Cady, a successful businessman, owned a three-story livery stable across the street from the house. Cady also owned another stable called the Eclipse, located in what is now Cady Hills. He eventually owned a hotel and one of the first plumbing businesses in Columbus.

Arbor House, so named for the antiques business of current owners Michael and Sheila Jessyl, is obviously the home of serious antique collectors. Important Victorian antiques inherited from five generations of their families and a museum-like collection of Old Paris porcelain are displayed throughout the colorful, tasteful home.

The Jessyls came to Columbus from Memphis and experienced love at first sight when they saw the two-story house. The Arbor House is open for tours by appointment.

Located at 518 College Street, it is listed on the National Register of Historic Places.

Arbor House Dining Room

The Berry Home c.1843
Bluecutt Road

Back in the 1840s, the Berry Home was a farm in the country. It is now in the city limits and no longer a farm, though the home and acreage still have the appeal of a country manor. The home is a square, Greek Revival cottage style, with a hipped roof and a widow's walk and a porch adorned by double columns. Many interesting additions and alterations through the years make it completely unique. The four original rooms are connected by a wide central hall, with a stairway rising from the hall. An original kitchen was detached, but an addition in the 1920s joined the kitchen to the house.

During a renovation in the late 1970s, original hand-hewn cypress beams were discovered in the kitchen ceiling. The beams are in use today, though they're placed in the opposite direction of the previous placement. Original pine flooring is still in place, and the old brick fireplaces are topped by pine mantels.

Wide crown moldings and the interior design talents of Lounora Berry create a wonderful atmosphere for the Berry family home. Lounora's father was in the furniture manufacturing business, also her husband Charles and their sons. Lounora has lived in the home much of her life. She remembers pleasant times of riding horses across the hills and pastureland. Before her father, Russell Johnston, bought the home, it was owned by the Lindamood family, who bought it from the Whitfields.

The house was probably begun in the early 1840s by William Whitfield, according to information pieced together from the old cemetery on the grounds. One marker shows that Whitfield, who was born in Lenoir County, North Carolina in 1787, died here in 1854 and is interred in the old crumbling brick and vine-covered cemetery. Census records for Lowndes County, Mississippi, 1860, show that a Whitfield son and family had real estate worth $55,000, which was the home, out buildings, and acreage.

The Berry Home sits serenely back from Bluecutt Road, just off Military Road, which is also Hwy. 12.

Whitehall c.1843
607 Third Street South

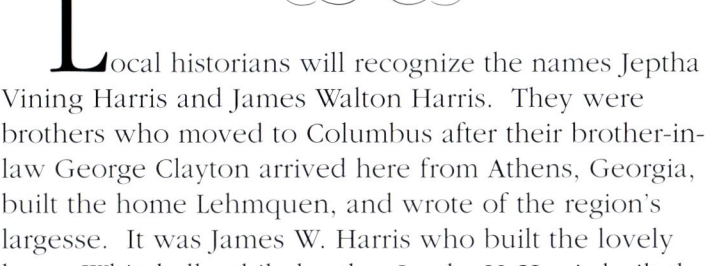

Local historians will recognize the names Jeptha Vining Harris and James Walton Harris. They were brothers who moved to Columbus after their brother-in-law George Clayton arrived here from Athens, Georgia, built the home Lehmquen, and wrote of the region's largesse. It was James W. Harris who built the lovely home Whitehall, while brother Jeptha V. Harris built the equally lovely White Arches across the street.

The Harrises were planters, and the money gleaned from the farms built their homes. The pillared Greek Revival Whitehall is symmetrical in design. The house originally covered a city block with terraced gardens, servants' quarters, and stables. This particular house has also been called "Georgian Colonial" in style.

James and Martha Harris had seven children. Their eldest daughter died in the house at age 15; their three sons served the Confederacy during the Civil War. Two were captured but later escaped. Young "Bud" Harris was only 16 when he went to fight for "the Cause." After his escape from a Union prison, he made his way back to his beloved Whitehall. When the federal soldiers came to search for him, his mother hid him in the attic until the Yankees departed. Bud then rejoined his Confederate compatriots.

Later in the war, Whitehall was one of the houses in Columbus that was used as a hospital for Confederate soldiers. An interesting event occurred that has been told many times. While soldiers were convalescing at Whitehall, Martha Harris ministered to them daily, and she also served as president of the Soldier's Relief Association, which required her presence at all the local hospitals.

According to legend, a "Yankee boy" who had been taken prisoner was deathly ill with typhoid fever. A surgeon advised Martha that the young soldier from Maine could not last long, for he was delirious to the point of thinking that Mrs. Harris was his mother. Once, she heard him whisper, "Pumpkin pie." She asked him to repeat the statement, and heard "Pumpkin pie" again. The doctor said the boy was dying, so Martha rushed home and baked him a pumpkin pie. The next day, he was better, and he asked for more pie. Long after he recovered from his serious ailment, the young soldier credited the pie and the "kind Southern lady" with saving his life.

Later, Whitehall was purchased by Thomas Hardy, husband of Mrs. Sally Bailey Hardy and granddaughter of James T. Harris. Thus, the home remained in the Billups/Hardy family for five generations. The grand old mansion was purchased by Dr. and Mrs. Julian Boggess, Jr. in 1956. They modernized, but kept the architectural character intact. Whitehall remains in the Boggess family; it is located at 607 Third Street South.

The Haven c.1843
315 Second Avenue North

The original home was built by Isaac and Thomas Williams, both "free men of color" who bought the lots and began building in 1843. The original house consisted of four rooms—two up and two down, with the stairways located outside the porches. The Williams brothers, one a laborer and the other a blacksmith, came to the area from South Carolina and both were considered prosperous. They had their own blacksmith shop on the corner of the property, now known as The Haven.

Though the actual year of construction is unknown, it is known that the house was standing in 1849 because it is illustrated in Oscar Keeler's "Map of Columbus, Mississippi," issued in 1849. The house is a raised cottage with brick basement and frame principal floor, with handmade bricks used as re-enforcement; the walls are three-bricks thick. The chimneys are 35-feet tall and still stand perfectly straight, which attests to the construction prowess of the Williams brothers.

A broad, low gable roof, similar to homes in South Carolina's Low Country, covers a full-width gallery across the front. The facade contains three bays on both the basement and upper levels. The basement area has simple moldings while the principal floor features early Greek Revival moldings. The house has been remodeled over the years, but still bears a strong resemblance to the description of the Williams brothers' home.

In early 1851, Isaac sold his interest to Thomas, who then moved from Mississippi and turned over management of the property to a local attorney. In 1858, Nathaniel E. Goodwin, attorney for the estate of Thomas Williams, F.M.C., deceased, sold the house to Adam Gass. The house has also been known as The Williams-Gass House. William Steen, an immigrant from Denmark, bought the property in 1870 and added the easterly half of the present home. Much of the furnishings from that period remain in the home

Today this interesting house near downtown Columbus is the home of Frank and Ester Troskey, who bought and renovated it in 1974.

The Haven is located at 315 Second Ave. North.

The Blewett-Harrison-Lee Home c.1847
316 Seventh Street North

This popular public home —known locally as the Lee Home— has been the site of many festive occasions. Major Thomas G. Blewett had this fine Italianate home built for his family, and for posterity. The solid brick walls are almost three feet thick, and the bricks are locally made. Skilled craftsmen and artisans constructed the home, reputed to be at a cost of about $80,000, a very high price at the time even though it included dependencies.

General and Mrs. Stephen Dill Lee inherited the house from Regina Lee's mother. At their deaths, the house went to their son, Blewett Harrison Lee, an attorney who practiced law in Chicago. He sold the property to the City Schools in 1916. S.D. Lee High School was built nearby, with the existing house serving as the Home Economics building and the school cafeteria. In 1959, fire destroyed the school and damaged the house, but two groups organized to preserve the building.

Today, the Lee Home is managed by the Columbus-Lowndes Historical Society and the Preservation of Antiquities in Columbus and Lowndes County. On the second floor, the Florence McLeod Hazard Museum exhibits Civil War artifacts and a collection of period bridal gowns.

This National Register of Historic Places structure is located at 316 Seventh Street North.

Camellia Place c.1847
416 Seventh Street North

It stands to reason that Camellia Place is a work of architectural art, for it was the first home of architect/builder James A. Lull, formerly of Vermont. Early reports indicate that Lull built Camellia Place for himself and his family, then enlarged and embellished the same design for Riverview.

Mrs. Eugenia Morgan Moore, great, great aunt of present owner Jack Kaye, bought the house from Lull heirs around 1880. The new owner wanted to update and modernize her home, so she went to Chicago to purchase Victorian furnishings and design elements to replace the existing Greek Revival accouterments.

Change styles she did, with custom-designed mahogany woodwork, marble and onyx mantels, and a cherry handrail from the stairway that winds around to its final destination: the observatory — or cupola, or widow's walk. Window cornices are made of finely carved mahogany.

The tin roof and gutters are duplicates of the originals, though many originals are still in place, among them fine family paintings. An original painting by Sir Frank Salisbury hangs prominently at Camellia Place. The knighted artist Salisbury, who painted members of the British and French royal families, painted the portrait of Jack Kaye's mother from photographs.

The spacious and gracious Camellia Place is located at 416 Seventh Street North.

The Amzi Love Home c.1848
305 Seventh Street South

Amazingly, the Amzi Love home is still occupied by descendants of the original builder. According to legend, when the young lawyer Amzi Love asked for the hand of Miss Edith Wallace, he then had local builder James Lull help design the cottage-style home.

In keeping with the prominent trend of the day, the Amzi Love combines traces of many styles: mainly Italianate, with Greek Revival and Gothic Revival features. The result is a distinctly original style that denotes warmth and charm, beginning with openwork columns and arches.

Enter the Amzi Love through a door bordered by sidelights and transom boasting Venetian glass panes. The colors of the unusual diamond-shaped panes are ruby, cobalt, green and amber, which offset the gracefully curved walnut staircase in the front hall.

Luckily for historians who honor authenticity, original treasures are abundant at Amzi Love. The parlor holds two Empire secretaries filled with family heirlooms, from silver thimbles to Meissan figurines to a pewter inkwell. The parlor is illuminated by the original crystal chandelier. Outside, the original smokehouse and dairy are still standing.

The Amzi Love is now the home of seventh generation descendant, R. Sidney Caradine, III and his wife Brenda. Sid left a career in the stock market in Memphis to return to the "old home place." The ancestral home is also a popular bed-and-breakfast inn, one that has played host to nationally known media personalities and writers.

Located at 305 Seventh Street South, the Amzi Love is listed on the National Register of Historic Places.

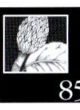

Errolton c.1848
216 Third Avenue South

If this gracious and grand Gothic/Greek Revival mansion was built as a "summer home," one can only imagine the grandeur of the permanent residence. Merchant William B. Weaver of Mobile built the home around 1848, complete with marble mantels, decorative colored glass, and some furnishings from Europe. For years, the house was known as "the Weaver Home."

Errolton, so named after the Bateman family bought it in 1953, dates back in name to Hay-Bateman ancestors in Scotland and later a family plantation near Charleston, South Carolina. The house is more romantic in appearance than many Columbus houses. Tudor arches with wooden tracery spandrels adorn the space between the tall, octagonal fluted columns on the portico. Red glass around the sidelights and transom creates a magical effect on sunny days.

According to Chebie Bateman, the red glass is on the front —the northern side— to create a rich, warm feeling. The blue on the back entrance symbolizes coolness.

Errolton features a distinctly classical interior, with double parlors, marble mantels, pier mirrors, and ornate plaster medallions. The lovely interior is a perfect backdrop for the fine antiques and family paintings.

This home is one that has an often-told ghost story, and the ghost is named Miss Nellie. Legend has it that around 1877, Nellie fell madly in love with a volunteer fireman named Charles Tucker. When he gave Nellie an engagement ring, she used it to etch "Nellie" in a glass window pane in the south parlor. She married her fireman in 1878. A few years later, he left Nellie and their daughter. To support the two of them, she ran a private school in a servants' house behind the big house. In her old age, Nellie rocked on the porch, recounting festive stories of her pre-Charles youth. At this time, the house began to fall into disarray.

Miss Nellie died in 1930. When the Bateman family bought the house and began renovation, they found the window with "Nellie" etched on it. Unfortunately, the original window was subsequently shattered by a falling ladder and had to be replaced. Later, as Mrs. Bateman first closed her new drapes, she found "Nellie" etched on the new glass, in the same place as it had been on the old window pane.

Errolton, at 216 Third Avenue South, is the home of the Douglas Bateman and Keith Gaskin families. It is listed on the National Register of Historic Places.

Bryn Bella c.1849
1822 Stinson Creek Road

Built around 1850 for William S. Cox —perhaps by local architect/builder James Lull— this house has been through many owners and name changes. Bryn Bella has been known as the Cox Home, Cedar Ridge Mansion, the Mennonite Home, the Uithoven Home, and the Ward Home, among many. Others thought to be owners include C.J. Bender, Leon Bell, Arron Shrock, Henry Ward, even Weyerhaeuser, who sold it to Mike Bradshaw. Whatever it was in the past, it is now Bryn Bella, named for a noted country home in the Vale of Clwyd in North Wales.

It is easy to see why people want this great country planter's home, for Central Casting could not create a more perfect-looking place for a film about the Old South. The floor plan is four rooms with a central hall. The joining of a two-story rear stair hall pavilion with a one-story dining room/kitchen wing forms a T-plan.

The Greek Revival house sits amid ten acres of lawn, stately timbers, fruit trees and blueberry bushes. Abundant natural light makes Bryn Bella especially bright and cheerful. The main south porch, one of five, is counter-balanced by two small rooms on the north side of the house, a feature believed to be unique in Mississippi antebellum homes.

Bryn Bella is now owned by former Ambassador and Mrs. Robert Pugh. He served with the United States Foreign Service in Chad and Mauritania; his wife Thelma worked as a nurse in third world countries, though she hails from New Duston in Northamptonshire, England.

Ambassador Pugh once said that many Europeans are fascinated with the American South because it is such a distinctive region in America. Indeed it is.

Bryn Bella is located at 1822 Stinson Creek Road, near the Columbus Air Force Base. It is listed on the National Register of Historic Places.

Riverview Staircase

Riverview c.1850
216 Third Avenue South

Riverview is a quintessential Southern mansion —stately, massive, and stunning. The house that is so imposing it is almost intimidating recently won the coveted 'National Historic Landmark' designation, which is no easy feat and considered quite an honor. It's an honor well deserved, for Riverview is indeed exceptional.

The architectural style is Greek Revival, though some say its exterior is similar to homes in Middle Tennessee. Riverview is certainly a masterfully constructed showplace. But no clue from the red brick exterior prepares visitors for the grand interior design and details. Enter the foyer, look to your right, see the coffered 15 feet 8 inches ceiling in the front parlor, and know that it exhibits the finest neoclassic plasterwork in the South, without a doubt.

Deep denticulated cornices and an amazing frieze border the ceiling's center panel, where an ornate medallion is guarded by winged angels' heads inside a foliated square. The dining room plasterwork is equally fine. Tall, sliding doors separate the dining room (originally the parlor) from the front parlor, and elsewhere in the house, a counter-weighted wall, which goes up like a window, increases or decreases the size of the room. When it was functional, this paneled cypress wall was raised into a pocket on the second floor. Throughout the house, fine antiques are highlighted by vivid wall colors and rich woodwork.

In the hall, a mahogany stairway rises gracefully and effortlessly to the fourth floor. On the way up, the visitor finds two twin ballrooms on the second floor, servants' quarters on the third floor, and the cupola on the fourth floor. The cupola, or observatory, is enclosed with stained glass windows of green, red, amethyst and blue, representing the four seasons.

Riverview represents the proudest work of architect/builder James Lull. He built the house as a residence for Colonel Charles McLaran. At the time of its completion around 1852, Riverview and its lawn covered an entire city block. The one-story former kitchen and cook's quarters is adjacent to the house, though it is now used as a guesthouse.

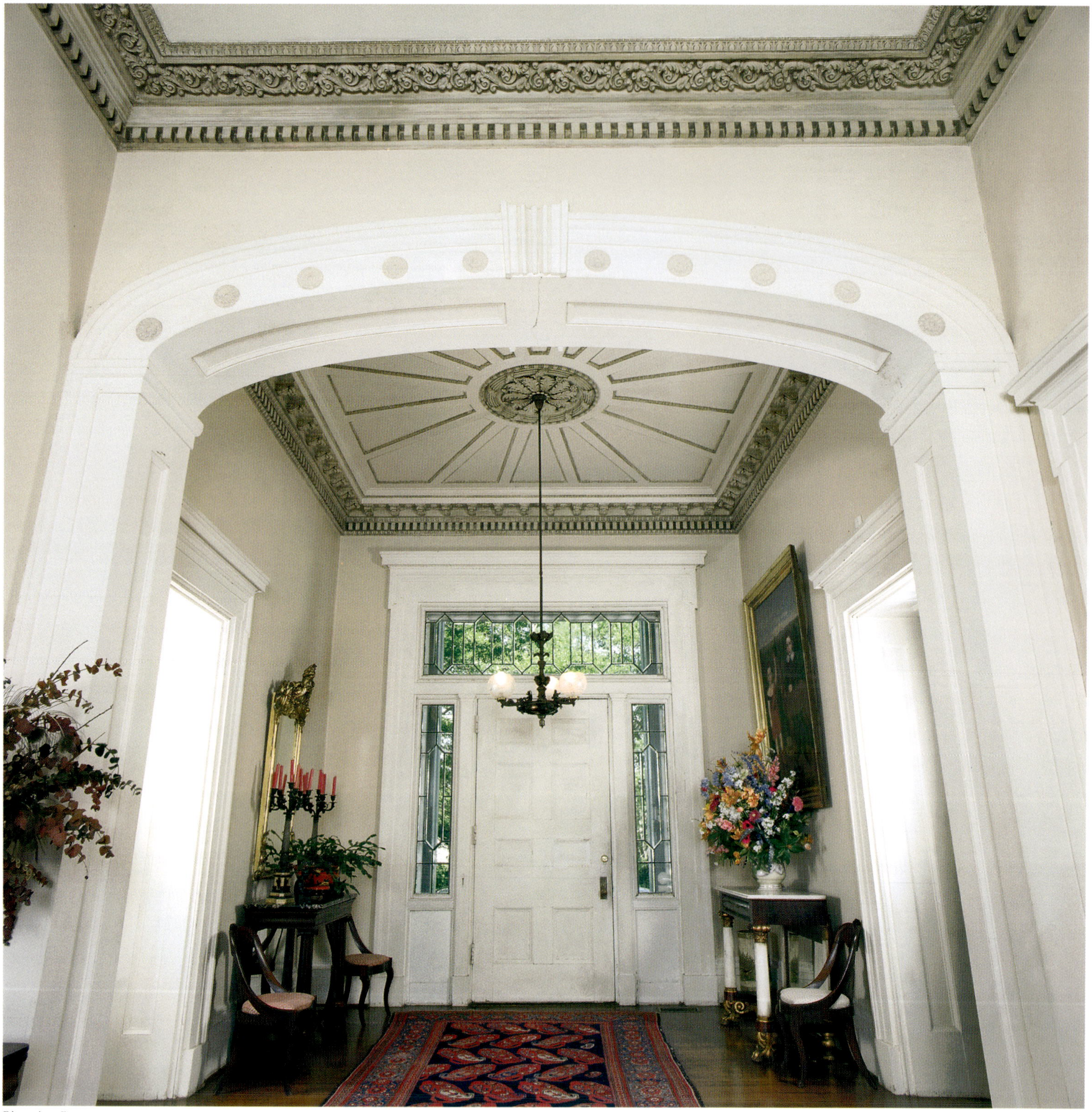

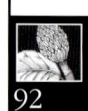

Riverview Foyer

In 1857, McLaran sold Riverview to John Gilmer, proprietor of the Gilmer Hotel. Gilmer's widow sold it around 1884 to W.W. Humphries, thus it was known as "The Humphries Place" for years. In the 1960s, Mrs. William Pratt Thomas, who lived directly across the street, bought the outstanding house to save it, for there was talk of razing it to build apartments. She sold Riverview to Dr. John Murfee and his wife Patty in 1971. Though Dr. Murfee is now deceased, Patty DeBardeleben still owns the home.

Riverview, at 514 Second Avenue South, is listed on the National Register of Historic Places and is a National Historic Landmark.

Riverview Parlor

Waverely Rotunda

Waverley c.1852
One Mile East of Highway 50

Waverley was once one of the largest plantations in the Deep South, and at the center of thousands of acres sat the most remarkable plantation house. The house was and is Waverley Mansion —still as spectacular as the year it was built. The house features an octagonal rotunda with a cupola —or observatory— that sits atop it like a crown. The 16 windows that surround the cupola serve as windows on the world to those who claim Waverley as their own.

The plantation was the domain of George Hampton Young, who built Waverley in 1852. Young came to the area as secretary of the United States Land Commission. His mission in Mississippi was to sell the land that the Choctaws had ceded to the federal government. Land was sold at $1.25 per acre, and it is believed that Young bought about 40,000 acres for himself. Young became a successful planter, and some reports show that he hired an architect from St. Louis, Charles I. Pond, to design his house. The design for Waverley was Greek Revival, an octagon set within a rectangle.

According to Waverley's owner, the house may have been patterned after a design attributed to the venerable Italian architect who honed his skills in the 1500s, Andrea Palladio. The modified "H" shape of Waverley is similar to that seen in some of Palladio's work.

When the Civil War broke out, all six of the Young sons joined the Confederate Army; all but one returned. Life was never the same after the war, though the Youngs went about the business of running the plantation and participating in the activities of the community. The National Foxhunters Association was founded at Waverley in 1893.

Young, a Columbia University-trained attorney, kept Waverley up in grand style until his death. At the demise of the last Young descendant in 1913, the grand old house fell into disrepair and stood vacant for fifty years, though it remained structurally sound. In 1962, the Robert Snow family from Philadelphia, Mississippi, saw the house and fell in love with it. Restoring it was a long and arduous ordeal that took more than 25 years, but today, Waverley is one of Mississippi's favorite showplaces and has been featured in prestigious national and international publications, and on the A&E television series, "American Castles."

Waverely Parlor

From the first floor, which also serves as a ballroom because of the spaciousness presented by the rotunda, two curving staircases lead to cantilevered balconies on the second, third, and fourth floors. The 16 windows around the cupola flood the rotunda with sunlight and cool air, when opened, and a most impressive visual impact anytime.

Waverley's owners are proud of the fine period antiques they have collected over the years, including pieces by Prudent Mallard and other noted furniture makers of the day. Splendid eighteenth-century and nineteenth-century pieces are in use at Waverley, including a Rococo Revival sofa and chair set by John Henry Belter and a Louis XV sofa and armchairs that are covered in Aubusson fabric. Among the original furnishings that remain are French ormolu chandeliers, pier mirrors, marble mantels, Venetian glass in the doors, and a walnut secretary. Today, Waverley Antiques is adjacent to the house, in the brick building that was once the plantation office.

Waverley is listed on the National Register of Historic Places; it is a National Restoration Award Winner, and a National Historic Landmark. The mansion is located about one mile east of Highway 50, between Columbus and West Point. It is open daily for tours.

Waverely Entranceway

A Waverely Bedroom

Snowdoun c.1854
906 third Avenue North

Two years after James Whitfield served the state of Mississippi as governor, he built Snowdoun, on the corner of Third Avenue North and Ninth Street. It was his home for ten years, after which time he sold it to Major John Marshall Billups in 1864. Snowdoun remained in the Billups family for more than 100 years. It is now owned by the Stephen Imes family.

The octagonal design of Snowdoun reflects the popularity of the designs of Orson Fowler, whose book about octagonal houses, *A Home for All*, was published in 1848. Snowdoun has an octagonal center hall with large rooms opening onto it. The rooms are square, with triangular closets originally designed to fit into the space where the square met the octagon. The massive, two-story, fluted columns are also octagonal, with the balconies and front galleries following this shape. Snowdoun initially had seven porches, each of which could be reached through jib windows, which also served as doors as needed.

Some say that Governor Whitfield had visited Thomas Jefferson's Monticello and liked the unusual, octagonal design of that spectacular house, completed in 1809 though it remained a work in progress until Jefferson's death in 1826. Whether from a book or a visit to Monticello, Governor Whitfield did himself proud when he had this house built.

Among the guests at Snowdoun over the years were Jefferson Davis, president of the Confederate States of America, CSA General Nathan Bedford Forrest, L.Q.C. Lamar, and the evangelist Sam Jones. Legend has it that when Jefferson Davis was a candidate for the United States Senate, he was visiting Snowdoun when a crowd gathered on the lawn to greet him. He was already in bed, but as an astute politician, he did not want to miss the opportunity of speaking to a crowd, so he got up, ran onto the balcony to say a few words, and forgot that he was attired only in his nightshirt. When he realized his error, he excused himself, then came back properly dressed.

Snowdoun has been completely remodeled by two families who owned it in the 1990s, the J.L. Teel family and the Tommy Howard family. The house is listed on the National Register of Historic Places. It is located at 906 Third Avenue North.

Sunnyside c.1854
324 Ninth Street North

It is likely that this house was built sometime after 1835 by William Sims, uncle of Stephen Brown. By the early 1850s, the small house and lot was in a dilapidated condition. Brown was anxious for a home of his own, so he bought the house and began making needed repairs and additions. He was, after all, a licensed attorney, though he found the work often unpleasant and not financially productive. He became a bookkeeper for Fay & Brother, a dry goods stores. Stephen Brown married Mary Frances Owen in 1851.

After the dry goods store closed in 1852, Brown was elected Judge of the Probate in 1853, at which time he moved his home further back from the street and added another room. In 1859, the front two-story addition was added, giving the home four 20-by-22-foot rooms plus a nine-foot-wide veranda. As probate judge, he served with distinction for four terms.

During the Civil War and the threat of an invasion by the Union Army, Judge Brown took records from the courthouse and kept them hidden in a secluded wooded area. He remained in seclusion and had food delivered by a trusted servant.

Wounded soldiers were housed in Columbus homes, one of which was the Brown residence. In 1862, while Mary Owen Brown was tending sick Confederate soldiers, she contracted typhoid fever and died. Two years later, Judge Brown married Mary Glass Shaeffer; they had six children. Judge Stephen A. Brown died in 1877, at the age of 54.

In 1976, the house was purchased by Jim and Helen Evans, who completely renovated the historic home and named it Sunnyside. Today the house is a graceful synthesis of Greek Revival and Italianate styles. The most notable exterior architectural feature is the two-tiered, lattice-arched gallery supported by delicate colonnettes. Interior features include a spiral staircase, jib windows, and wide, tongue-and-groove heart-pine floors. Period antiques are used throughout.

Sunnyside is listed on the National Register of Historic Places; it is located at 324 Ninth Street North.

Wisteria Place c.1854
524 Eighth Street North

This elegant old home looks as though it may have been a politician's residence, and indeed it was. William R. Cannon, who had the imposing house built for $7,000 in 1854, had been a Mississippi legislator and a state senator. He was elected president of the Senate and sometimes served as acting governor. Later, he served as president of the state Democratic Convention.

Unfortunately, Cannon contracted typhoid fever and died just after his 54th birthday. His funeral was the largest Columbus had ever seen. Jefferson Davis, United States secretary of war at that time, said, "I have lost my best friend. Cannon was the purest, truest, noblest, and best man I ever knew." Two years later, Cannon's widow married Samuel M. Meek, and political figures continued to gather at Wisteria Place.

Wisteria Place is a handsome example of the Greek Revival architecture typical in the South in the 1850s. The front facade is distinguished by the six square, free-standing columns and by the handsome balustrade used on the portico and the balcony above the entrance. The sidelights around the door are of crimson, cobalt, and purple Bohemian glass. Jib windows open onto the portico, allowing more space for entertaining.

The floor plan is typical of a planter's townhouse of the day. It boasts a wide central hall with one room opening off each side and a graceful staircase rising from the hall. Three large rooms stretch across the rear of the house, on the lower level, and the original kitchen is attached by a breezeway.

Owners Dr. Blair McIver and his wife Rusty added a gazebo, a deck and a pool. Keeping "period" in mind, they used old, hand-made brick to partially fence the pool. Wisteria Place sits on a slight knoll, at 524 Eighth Street North.

Rosedale c.1856
1523 Ninth Street South

Rosedale is not a hybrid, or eclectic, house. It is pure Italianate, with no borrowing from other styles and no indecisiveness about what it wants to be. The only non-Italian element is the transom over the front door, which is Federal and apparently a preference of Dr. William Topp, who had Rosedale built. The prominent details are the campanile, or bell tower; tall, arched windows, a canopied balcony, a piazza, and a somewhat flat roof.

When he built Rosedale, Dr. Topp knew what he wanted and how to get it. As a doctor, he knew the importance of research, and perhaps it was research that led him to the work of Philadelphia architect Samuel Sloan. Sloan's book, ***The Model Architect***, was published in 1852. Rosedale looks somewhat like one of the designs in the book.

It has been speculated that Samuel Sloan, who was in nearby Tuscaloosa, Alabama, while designing and overseeing the insane asylum there, may have had a connection with Topp and perhaps came to Columbus to help with the design of Rosedale. This, however, is speculation and has not been substantiated though it appears quite likely.

As the result of Dr. Topp's attention to detail and the possible collaboration with Sloan, Rosedale is recognized by architectural historians as Mississippi's finest example of Italianate architecture. When he built his showplace, it is believed that Topp brought in New Orleans craftsmen to design and furnish the interiors. Furniture included Rococo Revival and Empire pieces which were enhanced by walls in deep, rich shades of greens and blues and deep gold tones, all representative of the Mediterranean region that spawned the preference for "Italian villas" in the American South.

Dr. Topp, who never practiced medicine in Columbus, came from Nashville in the 1830s by way of Pulaski, Tennessee. He managed lands for his brother-in-law, served on a bank board and on the local college board, and became a planter and land speculator. The Topp family lived at Rosedale until 1904, when the Topp children sold the home to W.V. Grace.

Rosedale House

Rosedale's Gentlemen's Parlor

From 1940 to 1946, the Grace's daughter, Mary Grace Wood Anderson, lived at Rosedale about the time that Palmer Home children —who lived nearby— claimed to have seen lights in the tower room after having seen a shadow on the stairs. But the tradition is that Mary Grace never went to the tower.

In 1946, Richard Powell Fleming bought Rosedale from Mrs. Anderson. His son's family was in residence until 1993, when Mrs. Fleming sold to Terry and Deborah Stubblefield. The Stubblefields, who now live at Magnolia Hill, sold the home to Gene and Leigh Imes in 1998. The house and grounds provide a perfect place for their daughter Megill to play.

The Imes continue to upgrade their home, though keeping it within the period of construction is important to them. The fine antiques they've collected also reflect their commitment to the antebellum period. In fact, Gene and Leigh have acquired such a distinguished collection of mid-19th century furniture, experts have called it "a national treasure."

The work of German immigrant John Henry Belter, considered perhaps the finest Rococo Revival cabinetmaker of his time, is well represented among the Imes collection. Belter, based in New York City, reached his prime around the 1850s. He was best known for creating heavy, laminated rosewood Louis XV-style parlor and bedroom sets. Belter's signature style of laminating seven or eight layers of wood in alternating directions was indeed innovative.

Rosedale, listed on the National Register of Historic Places, is located at 1523 Ninth Street South.

Belle Bridge c.1856
200 Fourth Avenue South

This grand old mansion —a picture-perfect Greek Revival— was built in 1856 by prominent local lawyer Richard Evans. The house appears to have been designed by architect/builder James Lull, for it bespeaks the same quality that prevails in his other work.

The entrance is graced by a one-story encircling arcaded gallery supported by Doric columns. Inside, the rooms are spacious and gracious —updated in decor, but still consistent with the best of the antebellum period. Belle Bridge calls to mind a statement made by architect Samuel Sloan, in his introduction to the first volume of *The Model Architect*, in 1852:

"A man's dwelling at the present day, is not only an index of his wealth, but also of his character. The moment he begins to build, his tact for arrangement, his private feelings, the refinement of his tastes and the peculiarities of his judgment are all laid bare for public inspection and criticism. And the public makes free use of this prerogative. It expects an effort to be made, and forms opinions upon the result. We are beginning to see intellect admired more than wealth or power, and the one who builds a beautiful residence now, is as much respected as were the old Barons with their massive castles and troops of retainers."

Belle Bridge has made a significant historic contribution, too, for after the Battle of Shiloh, wounded soldiers were tended in this hospital/home. The home was later owned by Robert Betts, great-grandson of Colonel George Hampton Young, builder of Waverley Mansion.

Current owners, Dr. and Mrs. Albert Laws (Chance and Gail), have updated but not altered their home. Chance is a man whose interest in history includes period architecture, so it's a safe bet that Belle Bridge will continue to prosper under his astute eye.

Belle Bridge is located at 200 Fourth Avenue South.

White Arches c.1857
122 Seventh Avenue South

The elegant and eclectic White Arches may be the most individual house in the state, meaning that there's not another one like it. From its quiet perch on the corner of Seventh Avenue and Second Street South, White Arches inspires the curiosity of visitors to the town. Built in 1857, the house gracefully combines Gothic, Greek Revival, and Italianate elements, and the result is a most unusual and lovely house that is sometimes referred to as the best example of Columbus Eclectic architecture.

Perhaps White Arches' style reflects the varied taste of its scholarly builder, Jeptha Vining Harris. Harris came to Columbus from Georgia, where his family had been involved in the early politics of the South. According to research, Harris became a prominent planter in Lowndes County and served in the Mississippi legislature. With the beginning of the Civil War in 1861, he raised his own regiment of troops and rose to the rank of brigadier general in the army of the Confederate States of America.

Noted in the architecture are the Gothic arches that support the sloping metal roofs over the galleries. The center columns are large and rounded, characteristic of the Italianate style. The heavier, center columns support the central octagonal tower and its observatory on top. Four double doors lead from the second floor of the tower onto a wrought iron-fenced balcony, where solid brass balls top each of the corner posts in the gallery railing.

Greek Revival elements include the floor plan —with a typical wide central hall and large square rooms on either side— the dentil cornices and typical Greek key design in the millwork. Of particular note: handsome built-in bookcases made of walnut, which are original to the house. Other interior features have to do with doors —seven exterior doors on the first floor and eight on the second— with no knobs on the exterior side of most porches and balconies. A mahogany stairway in the hall leads to the upstairs rooms.

White Arches hosted one of the last of the "old time parties" ever to be held in Columbus. The party was held just at the outbreak of the Civil War, the night before the Columbus Riflemen left to fight for the Confederate cause. It was a festive occasion, because hopes were high for victory, but a sad one, too, because the young men were leaving.

Owners Ned and Sarah Hardin use period antiques throughout the lovely White Arches, located at 122 Seventh Avenue South. It is listed on the National Register of Historic Places.

The George Hazard Home c.1859
1006 College Street

Since this peach-colored antebellum is situated on the busy street that leads to the Mississippi University for Women, it gets its share of attention. Unfortunately for those who are interested in history, there's not been much written about this wonderful home. Perhaps that will change someday, for in this house lives George Hazard and family; George is a well-known local educator/writer.

It is believed that James Henry, an early settler who acquired wealth and prominence, built this house around 1858. This classic Italianate raised cottage is a one-story frame that features a Tuscan-columned portico and a hip-roof side extension. The pilasters are fluted, and the cornice brackets are accented by pendants.

The existing interior remains much the way it was, though extensive work has been done in the kitchen, and a new wing has been added to the back. The wing has been perfectly blended into the existing house, creating a pleasing effect and much more living space for the Hazard family.

The home is located at 1006 College Street.

Shadowlawn c.1860
1027 College Street

From the street, Shadowlawn creates an imposing picture of the real Old South. The six stately columns joined together by Gothic tracery; the red Bohemian glass sidelights and transom; the balconies; the wrought iron fence and swinging gate —how perfect can a grand old Greek Revival house with Gothic influences be? Driving by is just not enough. The house all but asks you to stop by and make a photograph, for at certain times of the day, when the light is perfect, this is a photo opportunity not to be missed.

Initially built by the family of a prosperous merchant, Shadowlawn's exterior would be classic Greek Revival if it weren't for the delicate Gothic influences, for it comes complete with a grand front portico, large fluted columns, and a side gallery. Jib windows, once used as doors, lead to the galleries.

In 1860, John W. Spears hired Hardy Stevens and his workmen to build his home. Back when it was built, according to legend, the name Shadowlawn was suggested by the flickering shade of the elm trees that lined the street. After his business took him out of town, Spears sold the home to John Stockard, who later sold to E.P. Odeneal. The Odeneals sold the house to the Patrick Mahon family, who lived there about 50 years. In 1925, the Mahon heirs sold Shadowlawn to T.A. McGahey; the McGaheys sold to Dr. and Mrs. S.B. Platt and family, and the Platts sold to current owner Charles Gaddis.

Gaddis, an Atlanta native, is a contractor by profession who has an astute eye for historic architecture and a commitment to honoring the integrity of the original design. His restoration of Shadowlawn included duplicating and replacing what needed replacement in the old section of the house, while keeping the new addition to his liking and lifestyle but still not losing sight of the fact that the property is historic. Other than the addition, the house will look like it did 100 years ago, only better.

Shadowlawn is Gaddis's third historic restoration project; the first in Columbus. The house is listed on the National Register of Historic Places; it is located at 1027 College Street.

The Colonnade c.1860
620 Second Street South

The Colonnade was one of the last grand houses to be built in Columbus before the Civil War. And after the war, grand homes took a back seat to survival.

Built around 1860, the Colonnade has a feature popular in homes built in Mobile, Alabama, in the mid-1800s —an asymmetrical entrance. Usually, Greek Revivals are built in perfect symmetry. Perhaps Dr. William Baldwin, a native Georgian, liked the Mobile architectural trend and instructed his builder to place the front entrance off-center.

The Colonnade is a large, two-story hip-roof frame house with a deep portico, tall pillars, a jigsawn balcony, and a bracketed cornice. The parlor features floor-length windows.

Earlier reports indicate that the upright framework of the house is put together with wooden pegs. The original pine flooring is in excellent condition, perhaps because of the resin in pine, which is thought to discourage termites.

On the site of the original kitchen, just behind the main house, sits a trophy room/den for homeowners, the William Sanders family. Serious gardeners will appreciate the lovely, well-tended formal gardens at the Colonnade, and its emerald back lawn bordered by majestic trees.

The house is located at 620 Second Street South.

Hamilton Hall c.1860-61
Corner of Third Avenue and Ninth Street North

Hamilton Hall is an Italianate townhouse that appears to have been built in two sections, one constructed in the 1840s and the others in 1860. The first section was more than likely a carriage house— some say a tavern— that was built about 20 years before former Mississippi governor James Whitfield bought the lot and had the villa constructed as a wedding gift for his son, Henry Whitfield, and his bride, Laura Young Whitfield.

The Italianate style of the mid-to-late 1800s was not as popular in the Deep South as elsewhere, but when Italianates were constructed, the architecture proved to be superb.

The young Whitfields sold the home to Marcellus Hatch in 1867, who later sold it to Richard E. Moore. Rumor has it that Mr. Hatch lost the house to Mr. Moore in a heated poker game. Records show that "...square 60, north of Main," became the property of Moore for $9000, "...half of which was paid in cash." The Moore family kept the big brick home until 1925, when it was sold to Mrs. Annie Hamilton and became known as Hamilton Hall. The Hamiltons were in residence until 1965. Annie Hamilton worked tirelessly in her garden, taking great pleasure in its beauty. Current owners, Dr. and Mrs. John Parker, share Mrs. Hamilton's passion for the gardens, which are indeed lovely.

Hamilton Hall delights the eye as an asymmetrical arrangement of lines and shapes, with brick walls, a symmetrical tower on the side, and a plethora of porches. When the second section was added to the existing structure in 1860, much pride was taken in the use of modern conveniences. "Speaking tubes" connected the first floor to the second; a bell system with a different sound for each servant was installed; and a water system was improvised, employing a large tank in the attic.

The Tommy Howard family bought the house and lived there from 1971 until 1981, with extensive renovation and interior design work done by Howard's wife at that time, the artist Eugenia Talbott.

John and Sherry Parker and family have owned the home since 1981. They have been carefully selecting and collecting appropriate antiques and furnishings. The renovation of Hamilton Hall and the restoration of the gardens continue today.

Hamilton Hall is on the northeast corner of Third Avenue and Ninth Street North, across from the octagonal Greek Revival Snowdoun.

St. Paul's Church stained glass window signed by Louis Comfort Tiffany.

A New Beginning

By the time Hamilton Hall was finished, the nation was at war. The years between 1835 and 1860, when most of the grand homes were built, were prosperous years of growth and development, thanks in part to cotton production. Change is inevitable, however, and it came to Columbus shortly after the halcyon years. Unfortunately, the South was ill-prepared for the changes wrought by the Civil War. The South seceded from the Union; the Southern states wanted to form their own nation and honor states' rights. The state known to be the hotbed of Southern separatism, South Carolina, led the secession on December 20, 1860, followed by Mississippi on January 9, 1861.

Columbian William S. Barry presided over the Mississippi Secession Convention in Jackson, where he and others known as "Fire Eaters" cast 84 votes to secede, with 15 voting to stay in the Union. These politicians were apparently passionate about their Southland, which was being threatened first by the federal government and then by the Abolitionists.

Popular Mississippian Jefferson Davis was the United States Secretary of War under President Pierce in 1853; by 1860 he was a United States Senator from Mississippi. The following is an excerpt from Davis's departure speech to the Senate, in which he defended the secession:

"...If you will but allow us to separate from you peaceably, since we cannot live peaceably together, to leave with the rights we had before we were united, since we cannot enjoy them in the Union, then there are many relations which may still subsist between us, drawn from the associations of our struggles from the Revolutionary era to the present day, which may be beneficial to you as well as to us. If you will not have it thus; if in the pride of power, if in contempt of reason and reliance upon force, you say we shall not go, but shall remain as subjects to you, then, Gentlemen of the North, a war is to be inaugurated the like of which men have not seen."

After the firing on the Union's Fort Sumter in the Charleston harbor, the South was never the same. General Stephen D. Lee, who is thought to have commanded the unit that fired the cannon, later became a resident of Columbus.

A New Beginning

Though Columbus was never invaded by Union troops, it was a devastating time nevertheless. The men were gone to war; the women were responsible for working the fields and feeding the families, and many times, for tending the wounded soldiers from nearby battlefields. The young soldiers were mostly Confederates, but in the smoke and confusion of battle, Federal soldiers were brought here to recuperate, too. The homes and churches were converted to hospitals, and the women of Columbus served as nurses.

When the soldiers died, they were interred in what is now Friendship Cemetery, and the ladies of the town later decorated the graves of Union and Confederate soldiers. That generous gesture in 1866 evolved into the nation's Memorial Day.

Though the Civil War was officially over in April, 1865, word did not reach Columbus until early May, when U.S. troops arrived to announce "Freedom Day." According to local legend, upon hearing the news of freedom, many house servants and former slaves walked away from their assigned duties and failed to show up for work the next day. Stories tell of the freedmen and women having a holiday that consisted of festive parades, drums, speeches, and "dinner on the ground" at a favorite gathering place, on or around May 8th. "Freedom Day" was celebrated for years afterward.

Meanwhile, since many of the white women of Columbus relied heavily upon household help and knew little about how to actually prepare a meal, they were desperate. The women of St. Paul's Episcopal Church, in the absence of their cooks, decided to serve luncheon at the church. The menu was limited to chicken salad and barbecue, easy enough to prepare even for the novice, they thought. So the families gathered, enjoyed the chicken salad and barbecue, and the Eight of May Luncheon proved to be such a success, it became a yearly event. Now, the "Ada May" luncheon —using the local pronunciation— is so popular, long lines of townspeople wait patiently to be served the traditional fare, and the annual event is a major fundraiser for St. Paul's Women of the Church.

The ensuing years of reconstruction crushed the collective spirit of the South. Gone were the days of grand mansions. A new South was emerging, and it was vastly different from the old. People in the town were looking for a better life, and that life began with education. In 1884, the nation's first state-supported college for women was founded in Columbus as the Industrial Institute and College, on the site of the old Columbus Female Institute, which opened in 1847. The college for girls earned a fine reputation as the best place for Mississippi families to send their daughters for a good education, for after all, it was cradled in the traditions of the Old South. The name was later changed to Mississippi State College for Women, and was affectionately called simply, "The W." The name was changed again, this time to Mississippi University for Women, but still "The W" prevailed. In 1982, the venerable college for women began admitting men.

By the end of the 19th century, people had adjusted to the lifestyle changes, and the women of the town turned their energies to literary pursuits. They organized the Shakespeare Club and the Century Club, reading circles, and musical societies, and the town became known far and wide as a place that offered a "cultivated environment." Shortly thereafter, the library came into being, and today the Columbus Public Library is one of the best in the state.

The Pilgrimage to Antebellum Homes

Around 1900, the lovely old homes of the mid-1800s were reeling and peeling, badly in need of repair. More hard times were in store with World War I and then the Great Depression. There was no money to keep the old houses up, so many were torn down. After the success of the Natchez Pilgrimage, which began in 1932, Columbus decided to capitalize on its remaining mansions, and the city's first Pilgrimage to antebellum homes officially began in 1940.

Pilgrimage was a festive event that required the work and dedication of scores of townspeople: those who lived in the homes and those who wanted to create a reason for people to visit the town, to help the economy. People came from all around to see the stately columned homes. They were amazed at the grandeur, and their enthusiasm gave Columbians a chance to see the homes in a different light.

Pilgrimage ceased after 1942 until the end of the war. When it began again, the townspeople were once again pleased to have a reason to celebrate, and, according to earlier newspaper reports, Pilgrimage was a city-wide event.

The tour of historic homes, still called "the Pilgrimage," continues to bring tourists to town for the major springtime event the first two weeks of April. It's the best time of the year to visit, for millions of spring flowers are in bloom, and there's a hint of a fragrance in the air. During Pilgrimage, the homes are dressed to the nines--with silver polished and shining, old crystal chandeliers glistening like new--and the most amazing fresh flowers arrangements adorning each room. Docents, or hostesses, are dressed in period costume, complete with hoop skirts and lots of lace. Add the mellifluous Southern voices that graciously greet visitors, and the Pilgrimage is like a trip back in time.

The same organization that sponsors the Pilgrimage, the Columbus Historic Foundation, also sponsors the popular Antique Show each fall. The fall event is accompanied by a well-attended Decorative Arts and Preservation Forum and a panel of nationally-known experts. For information on these events, contact the Columbus Historic Foundation at 662.329.3533 or www.historic-columbus.org.

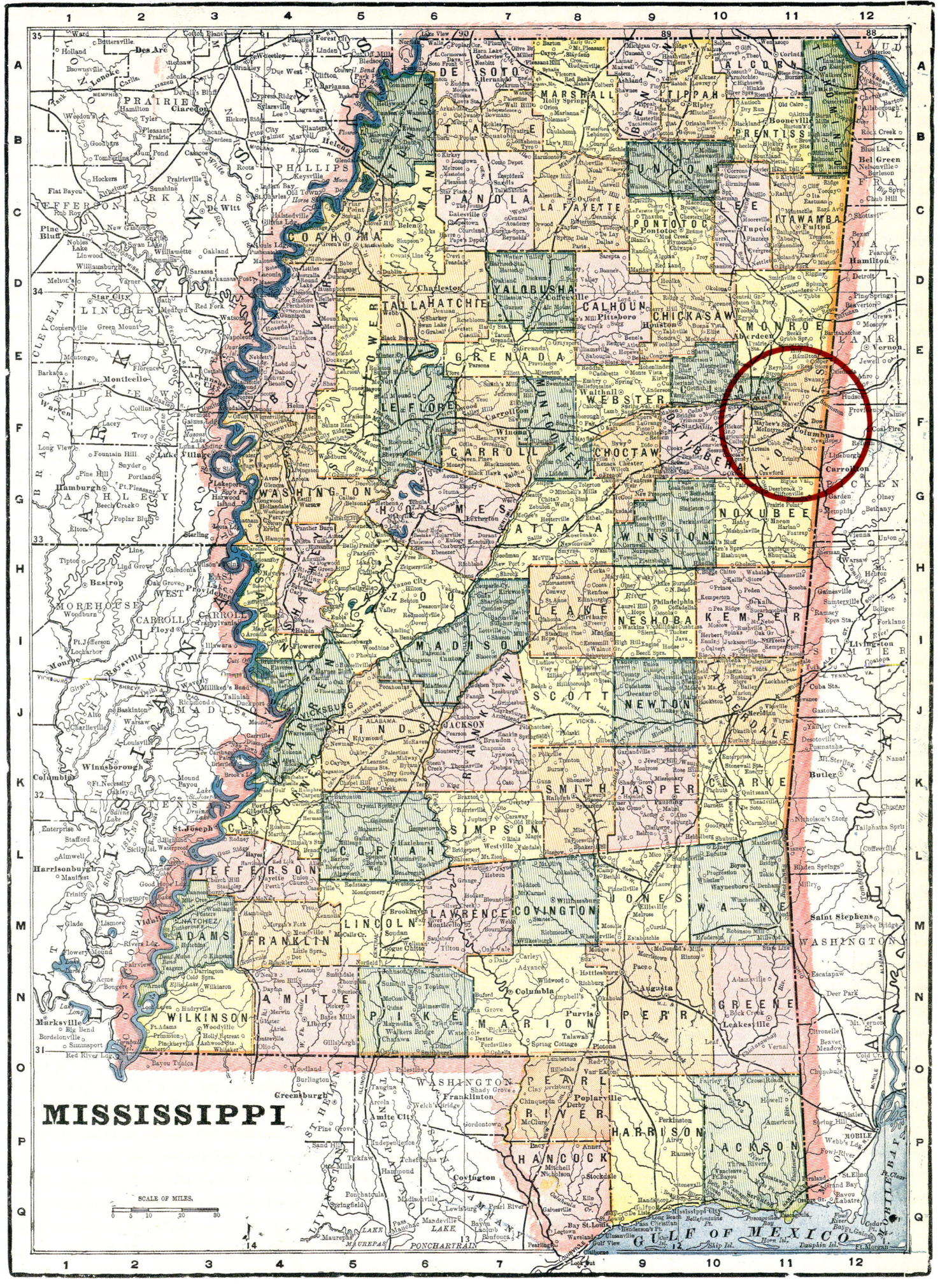

MISSISSIPPI

SCALE OF MILES.

The Tennessee Williams Welcome Center
300 Main Street

Apopular spot in Columbus is the Tennessee Williams/Columbus Welcome Center at 300 Main Street; it also serves as the Pilgrimage headquarters. The playwright Tennessee Williams was born in Columbus in 1911, while his grandfather, the Rev. Walter Dakin, was the rector at St. Paul's Episcopal Church. The young Williams family lived with Mrs. Williams parents in the current Victorian welcome center building, which was formerly the rectory and first home of the playwright. Williams won Pulitzers Prizes for his plays, *A Streetcar Named Desire* (1948), and *Cat on a Hot Tin Roof* (1955). He also won critical acclaim for such works as *The Glass Menagerie*, *The Rose Tattoo*, *Sweet Bird of Youth*, and *Night of the Iguana*.

Young Thomas Lanier Williams, later nicknamed "Tennessee," was an avid reader who was influenced by the works of Henrik Ibsen and Anton Chekov. In 1980, he received the Presidential Medal of Freedom. In presenting the prestigious award, President Jimmy Carter said, *"Tennessee Williams has shaped the history of American drama. From passionate tragedy to lyrical comedy, his masterpieces dramatize the eternal conflict of body and soul, youth and death, love and despair. Through the unity of reality and poetry, Tennessee Williams shows that the truly heroic in life or art dwells in human compassion."*

Tennessee Williams died in New York City in 1983. On the day following his death, the *New York Times* spoke of the line delivered by Blanche DuBois in "Streetcar" and said, under the heading..."Remembered Magic."

"No one who ever saw it forgot it: a woman with a broken mind taking the arm of the man who is to escort her to an asylum and saying with exquisite courtesy, 'Whoever you are, I have always depended on the kindness of strangers.'"

So might speak many of the historic homes in Columbus. For strangers have come into them in their time of need, restored and mended them, and passed them on to others to enjoy. And yes, for the most part, the manners of the Old South are still practiced here, as genteel people continue to impart exquisite courtesy and kindness to strangers.